ILLINOIS MEDICAL MARIJUANA LAW

ILLINOIS MEDICAL MARIJUANA LAW

A Practical Guide for Everyone

by Bradley Vallerius

Author Bradley Vallerius is an attorney licensed by the State of Illinois.

Marley Leighton Publishing, Gillespie, IL
Printed in United States of America

ISBN-13: 978-0615915685
ISBN-10: 061591568X

Cover design by Ben Riley.
http://benriley.net

Information contained in this book is summary only. It may not be construed as legal conclusion or advice.

www.MedicalMarijuanaLawIllinois.com

Contents

Debilitating Medical Conditions

Registered patients in Illinois may legally use cannabis to treat the following conditions:

- Cancer
- Hepatitis C
- Crohn's disease
- Muscular dystrophy
- Tarlov cysts
- Syringomyelia
- Fibrous dysplasia
- Multiple Sclerosis
- Parkinson's disease
- Myoclonus
- Causalgia
- Sjogren's syndrome
- Interstitial cystitis
- Hydrocephalus
- Glaucoma
- Amyotrophic lateral sclerosis
- Alzheimer's disease
- Fibromyalgia
- Hydromyelia
- Rheumatoid arthritis
- Spinal cord injury
- Spinocerebellar ataxia (SCA)
- Tourette syndrome
- Dystonia
- Neurofibromatosis
- Lupus
- Myasthenia gravis
- Nail-patella syndrome
- Residual limb pain
- Human immunodeficiency virus (HIV)
- Acquired immune deficiency virus (AIDS)
- Cachexia (wasting syndrome)
- Spinal cord disease (including but not limited to arachnoiditis)
- Traumatic brain injury and post-concussion syndrome
- Arnold-Chiari malformation and syringomyelia
- Reflex sympathetic dystrophy (RSD)
- Complex regional pain syndrome (CPRS), Types I & II
- Chronic inflammatory demylenating polyneuropathy
  Section 10(h)(1) for all.

Registered patients may obtain up to 2.5 ounces of cannabis (or the pre-mixed weight of cannabis in medicine or edible baked goods) per 14-day period. *Section 10(a).*

INTRODUCTION

Subjects Covered:

- Highlights of Illinois' medical cannabis law

- Changing attitudes about cannabis as medicine

- New economic opportunities

- New risks for private businesses and employers

- Why this book is for you

Highlights of Illinois' medical cannabis law

With the enactment of its *Compassionate Use of Medical Cannabis Pilot Program Act*[1] on Aug. 1, 2013, Illinois became the 20th US state to legalize cannabis for medical use. The law will have significant effects in Illinois because it:

- Allows cannabis to be used by registered patients with "debilitating medical conditions."
- Establishes procedures for physicians to prescribe cannabis to patients who have these conditions.
- Creates an entirely intrastate industry anchored by two new types of businesses:
    -> Up to 20 cultivation centers for growing cannabis and making cannabis medicine.
    -> Up to 60 dispensaries for selling cannabis products to registered patients.
- Establishes rules governing the ways and places a registered patient may legally use cannabis.
- Enables businesses to protect themselves from legal liability for accidents caused by employees and customers impaired by medical cannabis.
- Is merely a 4-year "pilot program," which means the market could expand later if this initial venture proves successful.

---

1. Illinois Public Act 098-0122 (enrolled as House Bill 01).

Changing attitudes about cannabis as medicine

Medical science provides strong evidence that cannabis is often the cheapest and most effective treatment option for certain medical conditions. According to the preamble of Illinois' new law:

> "*Cannabis has many currently accepted medical uses in the United States, having been recommended by thousands of licensed physicians to at least 600,000 patients in states with medical cannabis laws. The medical utility of cannabis is recognized by a wide range of medical and public health organizations, including the American Academy of HIV Medicine, the American College of Physicians, the American Nurses Association, the American Public Health Association, the Leukemia and Lymphoma Society, and many others.*"
> Section 5(c).

Public opinion surveys show increasingly favorable attitudes about cannabis. Most recently, on October 22, 2013, *Gallup* claimed: "a clear majority of Americans (58%) say [cannabis] should be legalized."[2] Meanwhile newspapers, magazines, and TV programs[3] are introducing America to a medical cannabis industry that dramatically improves patients' lives while developing innovative new medicines and delivering real economic benefits.

Cannabis continues to be a classified as a dangerous restricted drug under the US *Controlled Substances Act*[4], but the US Department of Justice has given assurances that it will not interfere in Illinois and other states as long as they regulate their internal markets responsibly[5]. The ultimate hoped for solution is a new federal law modernizing the old

2. "For First Time, Americans Favor Legalizing Marijuana," *Gallup*, Oct. 22, 2013.
3. "The Challenges of Starting Up in the Controversial Medical Marijuana Industry," *Entrepreneur*, June 6, 2013; "How to Invest in Dope," *New York Times*, June 25, 2013; "Medical Marijuana: Will Colorado's "green rush" last?" *CBS News, 60 Minutes,* Oct. 21, 2012; "Weed," *Special Report by Dr. Sanjay Gupta, CNN,* Aug. 2013.
4. 21 U.S.C. 801.
5. "Memorandum for All United States Attorneys; Guidance Regarding Marijuana Enforcement," Deputy Attorney General James M. Cole, Aug. 29, 2013.

classification of cannabis. But given the current state of US Congress, such a solution may be years away, even if it has clear popular support of the American people.

New economic opportunities

Illinois' medical cannabis law creates a new type of business called a cultivation center, which is envisioned as a massive industrial facility for growing cannabis plants and making cannabis medicine. The law also creates a second new type of business called a dispensary, which is like a retail store or pharmacy where registered patients and caregivers can buy cannabis products. The law requires cultivation centers to be spread throughout the state so that no district of the Illinois State Police contains more than one cultivation center. Dispensaries must be spread out so that every patient in Illinois has reasonable access to one. Jobs and other economic opportunities will therefore be created throughout the entire state.

For example, cultivation centers and dispensaries may tap into local communities to fulfill their need for:

- Architects, engineers, facilities designers
- Cultivators, horticulturists, others with growing expertise
- Accountants, bankers
- Security
- Transportation of products
- Equipment and maintenance
- Industrial goods and services
- Packaging and inventory supplies
- Laboratory technicians
- Operational managers, business consultants
- General independent contracting and labor
- Lawyers, lobbyists, communications agencies
- Other skilled professionals and general staffing

New risks for private business and employers

Illinois' medical cannabis law has significant consequences even for businesses that are not involved in the medical cannabis industry. Thousands of Illinois residents obtaining the right to use medical cannabis means many more people potentially becoming impaired and then causing accidents at work or in other places of business. The law helps employers, business owners, and other parties by allowing them to protect themselves from legal liability to some degree for accidents caused by patients impaired by medical cannabis. Employers, for example, have the right to make reasonable workplace policies restricting or altogether prohibiting the use of cannabis at work. Universities and landlords enjoy similar protections.

Why this book is for you

This book was written for anyone who is curious about what Illinois' new medical marijuana law means. The goal in writing it is to give a basic outline of the law in a way that everyone can understand. The book explains the basic rules for patients, physicians, private businesses, the general public, and the newly created medical cannabis industry.

This book can help you think about:

- How to become registered as a cardholder, if you're potentially a patient.

- How to invest, participate in, or provide goods and services to a cultivation center or dispensary, if you seek economic opportunity.

- How to legally prescribe cannabis, if you're a physician.

- How to advise clients and begin research, if you're a business or legal professional.

- How to attract or repel cultivation centers and dispensaries, if you're a local government official.

- ... and more, much more.

Regulation of The Medical Cannabis Industry

Subjects Covered:

- Adopting regulations

- Becoming a cultivation center or dispensary

- Four-year pilot program

- Illinois Department of Agriculture

- Illinois Department of Financial and Professional Regulation

- Illinois Department of Public Health

- Illinois State Police

The *Compassionate Use of Medical Cannabis Pilot Program Act*[6] was signed into law Aug. 1, 2013. It creates an entirely new intrastate industry focused on security and transparency in the production and distribution of cannabis. Only patients with specific debilitating medical conditions can become authorized to use cannabis. Registration and verification procedures ensure cannabis is purchased only by registered patients and their caregivers.

All functions related to growing cannabis and making cannabis medicine must occur at facilities which the law calls cultivation centers. Up to 20 cultivation centers may become authorized to operate-- one in each district of the Illinois State Police. The rights to operate these new businesses will be awarded through an application process beginning as soon as the Department of Agriculture can adopt appropriate regulations.

The law also creates up to 60 dispensaries, which are the exclusive store outlets where cannabis and cannabis medicine can be sold to registered cardholders. The law requires dispensaries to be dispersed so that every prospective patient throughout the state has "reasonable"

6. Illinois Public Act 098-0122 (Enrolled as House Bill 01).

access to one. Illinois' Department of Financial and Professional Regulation has authority to adopt regulations for dispensaries and will conduct the application process to award the rights to operate them.

Adopting Regulations

The law firmly establishes the size, structure, and general mechanics of Illinois' intrastate medical cannabis industry. But additional, more highly technical rules for cultivation centers, dispensaries, patients, physicians, and more are still needed. Authority for fleshing out these additional rules is granted to three administrative agencies of the Illinois government which have expertise in related subjects. The Department of Agriculture will develop rules for cultivation centers, the Department of Financial and Professional Regulation will develop rules for dispensaries, and the Department of Public Health will develop rules for patients and physicians. The Department of Public Health will also develop rules for safe food handing at cultivation centers that produce edible cannabis products such as cookies, brownies, and other food items.

Regulatory drafting period
Though already enacted, the law does not take effect until January 1, 2014. *Section 999*. The effective date marks the beginning of a 120-day period during which each of the three administrative agencies must explore relevant issues and then publish a draft of proposed regulations. *Section 165(a)*. Generally the length of time it takes to develop regulations is within an agency's discretion and may be dependent upon the scope and difficulty of the subject. The process may be slowed if there is a need to coordinate schedules with other agencies and to accommodate scrutiny and questions from the general public. The law encourages the agencies to seek input from interested parties throughout the rulemaking process.

The law instructs the three agencies that:

> *"During the rule-making process, each Department shall make a good faith effort to consult with stakeholders identified in the rule-making analysis as being impacted by the rules, including patients or a representative of an organization advocating on behalf of patients." Section 165(f).*

First Notice

The law instructs the three agencies to file their first drafts of regulations within 120 days after the January 1, 2014 effective date. *Section 165(a).* The agencies submit completed drafts to the Joint Committee on Administrative Rules (JCAR), which is a committee of Illinois General Assembly Members who oversee the rulemaking functions of Illinois' administrative agencies. JCAR is responsible for publishing proposed regulations in the *Illinois Register*[7] so that they can be reviewed by the general public.[8] An agency's filing of draft regulations with JCAR is known as its First Notice.

If the three agencies are able to complete their drafts before the 120-day deadline, then their First Notice could be published sometime before May 2014. The First Notice period lasts a minimum of 45 days and a maximum of 365 days.

Second Notice

After a minimum of 45 days have passed since the filing of First Notice, an agency may file its Second Notice with JCAR. An agency may file the exact same draft without making any changes or it may revise the draft and notify JCAR of the specific changes.

Following the filing of an agency's Second Notice, JCAR must review the regulations to ensure compliance with the enabling law. JCAR may in its discretion decide to investigate any issue it discovers

---

7. The *Illinois Register* is published every Friday and available free of charge on the website of the Illinois Secretary of State. (www.cyberdriveillinois.com/departments/index/register/home.html).

8. JCAR encourages public scrutiny of regulations by inviting comments and criticism via written submissions to its website. (www.ilga.gov/commission/jcar).

or that is raised by any member of the public. Second Notice lasts a maximum of 45 days.

Final rules

JCAR decides the fate of regulations after they have been filed for Second Notice:

> • One option for JCAR is to certify that it has no objections, in which case the regulations can proceed for immediate publication in the *Illinois Register.*

> • A second option is for JCAR to approve the regulations while recommending that certain changes be made. The agency does not necessarily have to make these changes though.

> • A third option is to make a motion of objection. If JCAR makes an objection, then the agency must issue a formal response within 90 days, but afterward may still go forward with its regulations without making any changes.

> • In cases where 3/5 of JCAR's members believe the regulations pose a threat to public safety and welfare, JCAR may exercise a fourth option to suspend or altogether prohibit the regulations from going into effect.

If JCAR makes no objections to the regulations or makes only recommendations, then the agency that drafted them may proceed to publish its regulations in the *Illinois Register,* with or without accommodating JCAR's recommendations. Regulations can become effective immediately or after a delay of not more than 45 days since the filing of Second Notice.[9]

Inter-agency cooperation

The law suggests that the three agencies with rulemaking authority under the medical cannabis law should coordinate with each other

9. Illinois rulemaking procedures are found in the *Administrative Procedure Act (5 ILCS/100).*

rather than work in isolation. The law instructs that the agencies "shall enter into intergovernmental agreements, as necessary," to carry out their authority. *Section 15(d)*. Cooperating should generally help the agencies adopt rules that come into effect seamlessly and that are compatible with one another.

Compassionate Use of Medical Cannabis Fund

The three agencies are required to deposit all money they collect as application, registration, and renewal fees into a newly created Compassionate Use of Medical Cannabis Fund. The fund is to be used exclusively for the agencies' costs of implementing, administering, and enforcing the law and its subsequent regulations. Excess funds may be transferred to crime prevention programs. Otherwise, the fund is not subject to "any budgetary maneuver that would in any way transfer any amounts... into any other fund of the State." *Section 20*.

BECOMING A
CULTIVATION CENTER OR DISPENSARY

The law instructs the Department of Agriculture to oversee an application process whereby the rights to grow cannabis and manufacture cannabis medicine will be awarded to up to 20 cultivation centers. The law allows only one cultivation center in each district of the Illinois State Police. *Section 85(a)*. Similarly, the Department of Financial and Professional Regulation is instructed to oversee an application process to choose up to 60 dispensaries throughout the state that will receive the right to sell cannabis products to registered patients and caregivers. *Section 115(a)*.

The two agencies may begin accepting applications for cultivation center and dispensary registrations upon publication of their final regulations in the *Illinois Register*. The law already provides substantial guidance about the types of information an application must contain, but the agencies have discretion to decide the form of applications and to impose additional information requirements as they may deem necessary. *Sections 85(d)(13), 115(b)*.

Request for Proposals

Simultaneously with or shortly after publication of their final regulations in the *Illinois Register*, the Department of Agriculture and Department of Financial and Professional Regulation are both likely to publish a Request for Proposals or similar official document seeking applications from prospective cultivation centers and dispensaries. The agencies are likely to set a closing deadline after which applications will no longer be considered in an initial round of registrations. The agencies have reasonable discretion to decide how long they will hold the application periods open.

Application evaluation period

After the deadline for accepting applications has passed, the agencies may begin evaluating applications. The length of time it could take to evaluate all the applications may be heavily dependent on the number received. Evaluating applications should be expected to take several weeks at least.

First to market

Much time will have passed since the law's enactment on August 1, 2013 until the time the agencies have completed regulations, evaluated applications, and selected the winners of cultivation center and dispensary registrations. Naturally it will then take another significant amount of time before a registered cultivation center can complete the setup of its facility. Then, finally, the cultivation center can begin to plant its first crop of cannabis seeds, but of course it will take several more weeks before any plants are ready for harvest and sale to a dispensary.

FOUR-YEAR
PILOT PROGRAM

The *Compassionate Use of Medical Cannabis Pilot Program Act* is not intended as a long-term solution to Illinois' medical cannabis policy. The medical cannabis industry and the rules that enable it are authorized for only a temporary "pilot program" period lasting four years from the effective date of January 1, 2014. *Section 220.* Generally, a pilot program is a small-scale, preliminary experiment undertaken to learn about feasibility, size of market, social costs, social benefits, etc. A pilot program is not an end itself but merely an initial step toward a later full-scale project which integrates wisdom gained from the pilot program.

ILLINOIS
DEPARTMENT OF AGRICULTURE

Having expertise in agriculture, horticulture, cultivation and various related subjects, the Department of Agriculture is the natural selection to oversee cultivation centers.

Ag Dept. rulemaking authority

The law grants the Department of Agriculture power to make regulations concerning:

- Requirements for the oversight of cultivation centers.
- Recordkeeping requirements for cultivation centers.
- Security requirements for cultivation centers.
- Rules and standards for the "enclosed locked facility" of a cultivation center.
- Procedures for suspending and revoking the registration of a cultivation center or one of its agents.
- Rules for transporting medical cannabis from a cultivation center to a dispensary.
- Cultivation standards for cannabis plants.
- Testing standards for cannabis products.
- Quality standards for cannabis products.
- Application and renewal fees for cultivation center agents.
- Application, renewal, and registration fees for

cultivation centers.
- "Any other matters that are necessary for the fair, impartial, stringent, and comprehensive administration of this Act." *Section 165(c)(1-10).*

Ag. Dept enforcement duties

The law grants the Department of Agriculture power to enforce laws and regulations related to:

- Registration of cultivation centers.
- Oversight of cultivation centers. *Section 15(b).*

Illinois Department of Financial and Professional Regulation

Having expertise in protecting consumers and regulating licensed professionals, the Department of Financial and Professional Regulation is the natural selection to oversee dispensaries.

DFPR rulemaking authority

The law grants the Department of Financial and Professional Regulation power to make regulations concerning:

- Application and renewal fees for dispensaries.
- Application and renewal fees for dispensary agents.
- Oversight requirements for a dispensary's "agent-in-charge."
- Recordkeeping requirements for dispensaries.
- Security requirements for dispensaries.
- Procedures for suspending the registration of a dispensary or one of its agents.
- Application and renewal fees for dispensaries.
- Application and renewal fees for dispensary agents. *Section 165(d)(1-7).*

DFPR enforcement duties

The law grants the Department of Financial and Professional Regulation power to enforce laws and regulations related to:

- Registration of dispensaries.
- Oversight of dispensaries. *Section 15(c).*

ILLINOIS DEPARTMENT OF PUBLIC HEALTH

The Department of Public Health has substantial duties related to patients, caregivers and health care facilities. It also has authority over cultivation centers with regard to food-handling safety in the kitchen facility that is used for making baked goods, such as brownies, cookies, and other edibles.

Health Dept. rulemaking authority

The law grants the Department of Public Health power to make regulations concerning:

- Application fees for patients and caregivers.
- Form and content of patient and caregiver applications and renewals.
- Form and content of physicians' written certifications.
- The agency's procedure for considering patient and caregiver applications and renewals.
- Manufacturing of safe cannabis infused products.
- Reasonable rules concerning the medical use of cannabis at a nursing care institution, hospice, assisted living center, assisted living facility, assisted living home, residential care institution, or adult health care facility.
- "Any other matters as are necessary for the fair, impartial, stringent, and comprehensive administration of this Act." *Section 165(b)(1-7).*

Health Dept. enforcement duties

The law grants the Department of Public Health power to enforce laws and regulations related to:

- Establishing and maintaining a registry of qualifying patients and their caregivers.
- Distributing educational materials about the health risks of cannabis.
- Adopting rules to administer the registration program for patients and their caregivers.
- Adopting food handling requirements for cannabis infused products. *Section 15(a)(1-4).*

ILLINOIS
STATE POLICE

The Illinois State Police has significant responsibilities related to cultivation centers, dispensaries, and patients. The importance of the State Police is underscored by the law's insistence that there can be no more than one cultivation center in any State Police District. *Section 85(a).*

Background investigations of agents and patients

The State Police performs a function in preventing unsuitable individuals from participating in the industry or registering as a cardholder. The State Police conducts criminal background investigations of all chief officers, board members, and other agents of prospective cultivation centers and dispensaries, in addition to prospective patients and caregivers. *Sections 65(d), 85(d)(1), 95(a), 115(d).*

Review of cultivation center security plan

Prospective cultivation centers must submit the details of their security plan to the State Police for review prior to applying for a registration through the Department of Agriculture. *Section 85(d)(6).*

Random inspections power

Illinois State Police has explicit power to conduct random inspections of the physical premises of a cultivation center. *Section 105(h).*

Cultivation Centers

Subjects Covered:

- Functions of a cultivation center

- One in every State Police District

- Location restrictions

- Security

- Growing operations

- Infused products and edibles

- Laboratory testing facilities

- Packaging, labeling, and inventory

- Employees

- Principal officers and board members

- Applying to become a cultivation center

- Ongoing legal compliance

The law requires that all functions in the chain of production of medical cannabis must be performed at a new type of business called a cultivation center. It is not just the growing of cannabis plants that must be performed at a cultivation center, but also the making of cannabis infused medicines and edibles.

One of the law's major goals is preventing cannabis from being stolen or diverted at any point in the chain of production. The law therefore controls a cultivation center's personnel and operations through stringent security and recordkeeping requirements.

Functions
of a Cultivation Center

At its fullest potential, a cultivation center is an immense, multi-functional industrial facility where every function related to the production of cannabis and cannabis medicine is performed. This includes:

Growing cannabis plants: Planting, harvesting, and otherwise managing the growth of cannabis plants must be performed on the premises of a cultivation center and nowhere else. *Section 85(a)*. A cultivation center will likely grow many different genetic strains of cannabis and adhere to precise schedules for such things as lighting, watering, and harvesting.

Manufacturing cannabis-infused medicine: All activities related to the development and manufacture of cannabis products must be conducted on the premises of the same cultivation center in which the cannabis was grown and harvested. *Section 105(e)*. This entails extracting active ingredients from cannabis plants and infusing them into products such as pills, serums, ointments and other forms of delivery that are suitable for human consumption.

Baked goods and other food items: The law envisions a cultivation center may integrate a kitchen into its facility in order to make "Baked products infused with medical cannabis (such as brownies, bars, cookies, cakes), tinctures, and other non-refrigerated items..." *Section 80(a)(2)*.

Laboratory testing: Laboratory analysis of cannabis plants and cannabis products is essential to ensure consistency of dosage. All testing must be performed at the same cultivation center in which the cannabis was grown and harvested because cannabis may only leave a cultivation center if its destination is a dispensary. *Section 105(e)*.

Packaging, labeling, inventory: A cultivation center must have the capacity to package and store a large volume of cannabis products. Every product must be packaged in a legally compliant container with a legally compliant label. *Section 80(a)(3)*. Then it must be entered into a database system so that it can be located in inventory storage. *Section 105(f)*.

ONE IN EVERY STATE POLICE DISTRICT

Although one clause of the law grants authority to the Department of Agriculture to grant "up to 22" cultivation center registrations, for practical purposes it is not actually possible to grant more than 20. This is because another clause states that the agency:

> *"...may not issue more than one registration per each State Police District boundary." Section 85(a)*.

The effect of the latter clause is to limit the maximum number of cultivation centers to 20. As the map and table on the following pages illustrate, there are only 21 districts of the Illinois State Police, despite their being deceptively numbered up to 22. Also, one of the districts has only tollway roads in its boundary and is therefore unable to support a cultivation center.

The law encourages the Department of Agriculture to grant a cultivation center registration in every State Police District. The agency may not refuse to issue a registration if there is a "qualified" applicant in a district. *Section 85(a)*. An applicant would generally be qualified if it meets the minimum requirements of the law and the Department of Agriculture's forthcoming regulations. So for example, if there are five competing applicants in a State Police District, then the agency must award a registration to one and only one of them. If there is only one applicant in a district, then the applicant would be an automatic winner if its application meets the minimum requirements. Only if there were no applicants or only unqualified applicants in a district may the agency withhold a registration.

Image: Map of Illinois State Police Districts
Source: Illinois State Police (www.isp.state.il.us)

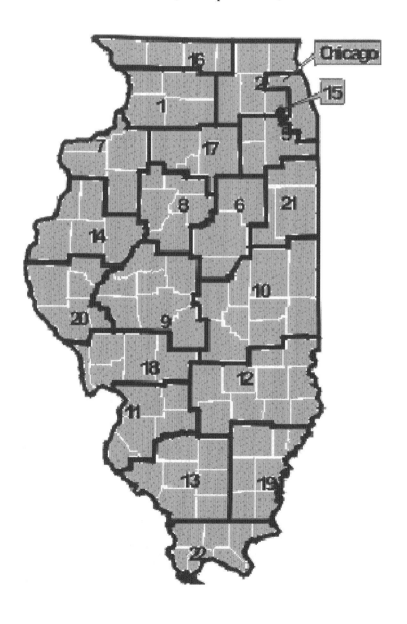

Table: Illinois State Police Districts and counties

Notice that District Chicago takes place of what would otherwise be Districts 3 and 4. Notice also, District 15 has only tollway roads in its territory. Hence there are only 20 State Police Districts in which a cultivation center may be located.

District 1:	Carol, Lee, Ogle, Whiteside.
District 2:	DeKalb, DuPage, Lake, McHenry
*District Chicago	**Cook**
District 5:	Grundy, Kendall, Will
District 6:	DeWitt, Livingston, MacLean
District 7:	Henry, Know, Mercer, Rock Island
District 8:	Marshall, Peoria, Stark, Tazewell, Woodford
District 9:	Cass, Christian, Logan, Mason, Menard, Morgan, Sangamon
District 10:	Champaign, Coles, Douglas, Edgar, Macon, Moultrie, Piatt, Shelby, Vermillion
District 11:	Bond, Clinton, Madison, Monroe, St. Clair
District 12:	Clark, Clay, Crawford, Cumberland, Effingham, Fayette, Jasper, Lawrence, Marion, Richland
District 13:	Franklin, Jackson, Jefferson, Perry, Randolph, Washington, Williamson
District 14:	Fulton, Hancock, Henderson, McDonough, Warren
*District 15:	**Illinois State Tollways**
District 16:	Boone, Joe Daviess, Stevenson, Winnebago
District 17:	Bureau, LaSalle, Putnam
District 18:	Calhoun, Greene, Jersey, Macoupin, Montgomery
District 19:	Edwards, Gallatin, Hamilton, Saline, Wabash, Wayne, White
District 20:	Adams, Brown, Pike, Schuyler, Scott
District 21:	Ford, Iroquois, Kankakee
District 22:	Alexander, Hardin, Johnson, Massac, Pope, Pulaski, Union

LOCATION RESTRICTIONS

The law imposes restrictions to keep cultivation centers at least half a mile away from residential zones, schools, and child care. The powers of local governments and the attitudes of local communities are also highly relevant considerations for prospective cultivation centers pondering the location of their facilities.

The following rules are explicit in the law:

> **Away from residential zones (2500 feet):** A cultivation center may not be located within 2500 feet (0.49 miles) of an area zoned for residential use.

> **Away from schools (2500 feet):** A cultivation center may not be located within 2500 feet (0.49 miles) of a pre-existing public or private:

> - preschool.
> - elementary school.
> - secondary school.

> **Away from child care (2500 feet):** A cultivation center cannot be located within 2500 feet (0.49 miles) of a pre-existing:

> - day care center.
> - day care home.
> - group day care home.
> - part day child care facility. (*Section 105(c) for all*).

Compliance with local zoning code and other ordinances

County, city, and village governments possess powers which they may use in friendly or unfriendly ways relative to a prospective cultivation center and its competitors. Most relevant is the power to make rules for land use and development, which includes zoning and rezoning. In some circumstances, a municipality may be able to adjust its zoning map to either prohibit or enable a type of business like a cultivation center. Local government may not, however, exercise power in a way that is inconsistent with the *Compassionate Use of Medical Cannabis Pilot Program Act. Section 140.*

A prospective cultivation center must decide upon its location by the time it submits an application to the Department of Agriculture. Along with its application, a prospective cultivation center must include a copy of the current local zoning ordinance for the area it wishes to occupy and provide verification that it would be in compliance. *Section 85(d)(11).*

SECURITY

A fundamental goal of the law is ensuring that no cannabis or cannabis products are stolen or diverted from the chain of production. The law imposes several layers of security requirements on cultivation centers to achieve this goal. Generally these rules are designed to prevent unauthorized entry onto the premises and to meticulously record every aspect of plant and medicine production from seed to sale. Further specifications concerning security may appear in the Department of Agriculture's forthcoming regulations.

"Enclosed locked facility"

A cultivation center's operations must take place in an "enclosed locked facility," defined as:

> *"a room, greenhouse, building, or other enclosed area equipped with locks or other security devices that permit access only by a cultivation center's agents or a dispensing organization's agent working for the registered cultivation center or the registered dispensing organization to cultivate, store, and distribute cannabis for registered qualifying patients." Section 105(d).*

The enclosed locked facility of a cultivation center must be accessible only to:

- Registered cultivation center employees.
- Department of Agriculture staff during inspections.
- Department of Public Health staff during inspections.
- Law enforcement and other emergency personnel.
- Contractors working on jobs unrelated to medical cannabis, such as installing or maintaining security devices or electrical wiring. *Section 105(d)*.

Security plan reviewed by State Police

A cultivation center must implement a security plan that satisfies the requirements of the law and the Department of Agriculture's forthcoming regulations. *Section 105(b)*. The law explains the basic components of a security plan but additional, more highly detailed specifications may appear in the regulations. *Section 165(c)(3)*. A prospective cultivation center must submit its proposed security plan to the Illinois State Police for review before it applies for a registration with the Department of Agriculture. *Section 85(d)(6)*.

The security plan must contain the following components:

- Facility access controls.
- Perimeter intrusion detection systems.
- Personnel identification systems.
- A 24-hour surveillance system to monitor the interior and exterior of the facility. *Section 105(b)*.
- A fully operational security alarm system. *Section 165(c)(3)*.

The 24-hour surveillance system must be accessible in real-time to the Department of Financial and Professional Regulation[10] and authorized law enforcement officers. *Section 105(b)*.

---

10. The law states that the Department of Financial and Professional Regulation rather than the Department of Agriculture shall have access to a cultivation center's surveillance system. *Se ction 105(b)*.

Secure transportation of cannabis to a dispensary

Security of transportation is immensely important because of the potential volume and value of cannabis products involved in a shipment from a cultivation center to a dispensary. The major concern is that deliveries make an attractive target for armed criminals. The law does not decide any rules related to the transportation of cannabis from a cultivation center to a dispensary, but it recognizes that such rules are vital to a safe, secure industry. The law specifically delegates authority to the Department of Agriculture to develop rules to ensure transportation is conducted safely and securely. *Section 165(c)(6).*

Employee management

Oversight of employees is a critical part of preventing theft and diversion. Prospective employees must undergo background investigations performed by the Illinois State Police before beginning work for a cultivation center. *Section 95.* Then once employed, employees must wear identification cards and adhere to rules governing the use of the cards. *Section 100.*

Recordkeeping

A cultivation center's ongoing legal requirements include keeping meticulous records of plants and inventory of products. *Section 85(d)(6).* Keeping good records helps the Department of Agriculture verify that no cannabis has been stolen or diverted.

Growing Operations

One thing the law makes unmistakably clear is that cultivation centers must be extremely thorough in their record-keeping of plant numbers and plant growth. Cultivation centers are expected to track every soil additive and every increment of cannabis growth "from seed planting to final packaging." *Section 10(c).* But beyond that, the law does not establish many rules related to growing and harvesting cannabis plants. The Department of Agriculture has reasonable discretion to adopt regulations to promote safety, efficiency, and other goals related to growing cannabis plants.

Specifically, the Department of Agriculture must make rules addressing:

"... standards concerning the testing, quality, and cultivation of medical cannabis." Section 165(c)(7).

Components of a growing operation

Appropriate planning for the following basic components is central to a successful growing operation:

- utilities
- water
- waste removal
- nutrients
- spacing of plants
- growing and harvesting cycles
- pest control
- lighting
- electricity
- soil
- additives
- ventilation
- facility design
- climate control

The law does not make explicit rules for these items, but the Department of Agriculture's forthcoming regulations may contain technical specifications for some or all of them. *Section 165(c)(7).*

"Cannabis plant monitoring system"

In order to achieve its goal of preventing theft and diversion of cannabis, the law requires a cultivation center to keep detailed records of every seed put in soil and every plant that emerges for harvest. More than that, the law requires a cultivation center to record incremental growth measurements throughout the entire life cycle of its plants. Reports reflecting this data must be submitted to the Department of Agriculture on a weekly basis. *Section 85(d)(6).* The law envisions a cultivation center will achieve this recordkeeping by implementing a "cannabis plant monitoring system."

A "cannabis plant monitoring system" is:

> *"...a system that includes, but is not limited to testing and data collection established and maintained by the registered cultivation center and available to the Department for purposes of documenting each cannabis plant and for monitoring plant development throughout the life cycle of a cannabis plant cultivated for the intended use by a qualifying patient from seed planting to final packaging." Section 10(c).*

The Department of Agriculture's forthcoming regulations may include further specifications about the use of cannabis plant monitoring systems. *Section 165(c)(7).*

Deciding which genetic strains of cannabis to plant

An important component of a cultivation center's business plan entails deciding how much of which particular genetic strains of cannabis to cultivate. Cannabinoids, a family of related active ingredients found in the cannabis plant, appear in different proportions across the many various genetic strains. For example, some genetic strains have relatively high levels of cannabidiol (CBD), which is particularly effective as a treatment for epilepsy, inflammation, anxiety, and nausea. And perhaps most significantly, CBD does not stimulate psychoactive effects.

By contrast, other genetic strains may be popular if they have high levels of tetrahydrocannabinol (THC), which binds to receptors in the brain. THC is an effective treatment for preserving neural function, reducing neuroinflammation, and stimulating new nervous system growth. THC is also known for causing psychoactive stimulation, hence it may be attractive to customers whose conditions don't necessarily require the particular cannabinoid. But for all the patients who do seek psychoactive stimulation, there may be just as many who would prefer to avoid it.

Ultimately deciding what genetic strains to plant may be a matter of business strategy for a cultivation center, influenced at least partly by market demand. A registered cultivation center may wish to plant a broad range of genetic strains or it might wish to focus on a narrow range of popular and effective choices. The law makes no rules distinguishing between genetic strains.

Pesticides

A cultivation center must comply "with all State and federal rules and regulations regarding the use of pesticides." *Section 105(k).*

Infused Products and Edibles

Technically the law does not require cultivation centers to manufacture cannabis infused products, which can take the form of pills, serums, ointments, lozenges, etc. But a cultivation center is the only place where these particular items can legally be made. *Section 80.* It means that in addition to becoming masterful at growing and harvesting cannabis plants, a cultivation center could establish a substantial market presence by developing its own unique and attractive medicines and food products.

Infused medicine and edible baked items are sometimes a more preferred treatment option for patients than smoking cannabis because different effects are generally experienced when a patient consumes cannabis by ingestion rather than smoking. And additionally because some people simply do not like smoking.

The field of cannabis infused products is actually a dynamic industry unto itself, with tremendous room for growth and innovation. Illinois cultivation centers are blessed that they are the only organizations in the state who may venture into the market. But they are also cursed because they must develop their own infused products divisions in-house and from scratch, rather than simply electing to export their cannabis to an offsite partner.

> **Varying forms of delivery:** One way cannabis-infused products can vary is in the form of delivery. For example, producers in other medical marijuana states provide cannabis medicine in the form of tablets, capsules, serums, ointments, lozenges, etc. These products can be varied further by using different flavors and other ingredients. For example, a cannabis infused serum that is administered

by spraying it under the tongue might be available
in a both a citrus and a peppermint flavor.

Varying dosages: Another way cannabis-infused products
can vary is in their dosage. This includes varying the
particular formula of cannabinoids in a product as well as
varying the strength of the product. For example, a
producer might develop a line of capsule products
featuring three different formulas of cannabinoids:
One formula could be high in THC relative to CBD, the
second formulat could be high in CBD relative to THC,
and the third formula could be a fair mix of THC and
CBD. These three different formulas could then be made
available in capsules of 25 mg strength or 50 mg strength.

Pre-mixed weight

"Pre-mixed weight" refers to the weight of cannabis used to make
a cannabis infused product or edible. Compared to the amount of
cannabis that must be smoked to get the intended effect, a substantially
larger amount of cannabis is needed to produce infused products and
edibles. The law's adequate supply of 2.5 ounces is much more than
any one patient could smoke by himself in a 14-day period. But with
regard to the pre-mixed weight of infused-products, 2.5 ounces is a
much more appropriate limit.

Specific rules for cannabis-infused products

The law imposes some basic rules on the cannabis-infused products
operations of cultivation centers. Additional rules may appear in
the Department of Agriculture and Department of Public Health's
forthcoming regulations. *Sections 165(b)(4), 165(c)(8).*

No refrigerated or hot-held items: Cultivation
centers may not make infused products or edible foods
that require refrigeration or hot-holding. This is "due
to the potential for food-borne illness." *Section 80(a)(1).*

Baked goods and tinctures ok: A cultivation center may make "baked products infused with medical cannabis such as brownies, bars, cookies, cakes), tinctures, and other non-refrigerated items." *Section 80(a)(2)*

Individually wrapped: All items must be individually wrapped at the original point of preparation. *Section 80(a)(3)*.

Legally compliant labeling: Every individually wrapped package must contain a label that complies with Illinois' *Drug and Cosmetic Act.*[11] *Section 80(a)(3)*.

Approved employees: Cannabis infused products must be prepared by an approved staff member of a cultivation center. *Section 80(a)(5)*. Rules covering the approved staff member may appear in forthcoming regulations. *Section 165(b)(4)*.

Health Department Inspections: The Illinois Department of Public Health has operational supervisory authority over cannabis infused products, which it shall exercise by deploying food service sanitation managers. *Section 80(a)(6)*.

Health Department authority over edibles

Because of its expertise in matters of consumer health and safety, the Department of Public Health receives authority to oversee cultivation centers' edible products operations.

In addition to adopting regulations, the agency has broad inspection powers to:

> *"...at all times enter every building, room, basement, enclosure, or premises occupied or used or suspected of being occupied or used for the production, preparation, manufacture*

---

11. 410 ILCS 620/.

for sale, storage, sale, distribution or transportation of medical cannabis edible products, to inspect the premises and all utensils, fixtures, furniture, and machinery used for the preparation of these products. "Section 80(b).

LABORATORY TESTING FACILITIES

A laboratory for analyzing cannabis plants and cannabis products should be an essential component of a cultivation center. Proper laboratory management enables a cultivation center to ensure that its products have consistent quality and dosage. Laboratory analysis is also an integral part of developing new products. Even if a cultivation center has no intention of manufacturing infused products and edibles, a laboratory is still an indispensible part of monitoring harvested crops to ensure consistent ratios of desired cannabinoids.

The law makes no rules governing the operation of a cultivation center's laboratory facility, but the Department of Agriculture is instructed to adopt rules covering "testing" and "quality" of medical cannabis. *Section 165(c)(7).*

Packaging, Labeling, and Inventory

Every medical cannabis product must be packaged in a sealed, tamper-resistant container in a way that ensures safety for human consumption. Packages must contain labels that display necessary warnings and ingredient information. Then after a product is packaged, it must be entered into a data collection system so that its location can be pinpointed in inventory.

"Medical cannabis container"

The law requires cultivation centers to package buds of cannabis in a labeled "medical cannabis container," defined as:

> "...a sealed, traceable, food compliant, tamper resistant, tamper evident container, or package used for the purpose of containment of medical cannabis from a cultivation center to a dispensing organization." Section 10(n).

This rather broad definition seems to allow cultivation centers some flexibility and discretion in deciding what types of container options to use. For example, safety-sealed plastic pouches and medicine bottles might both be valid options. The Department of Agriculture may make further rules concerning medical cannabis containers. *Section 165(c)(8).*

Labeling

For general health and safety purposes, it is important to provide labels which notify patients and anyone else who could come into contact with a product about its contents. The labels of medical cannabis infused products must give an explicit warning about the risks of using cannabis, in addition to such things as dosage and strength. Labels must also conform to the requirements of Illinois' Food, Drug, and Cosmetic Act[12]. *Section 80(a)(3).* The Department of Public Health may adopt further regulations addressing labeling requirements. *Section 165(b)(4).*

The following information must appear on the label of every cannabis infused product or edible:

- Name and address of the cultivation center where the product was manufactured.
- Common or usual name of the product.
- "All ingredients of the item including any colors, artificial flavors, and preservatives, listed in descending order by predominance of weight shown with common or usual names."

---

12. 410 ILCS 620/.

- The phrase: "This product was produced in a medical cannabis cultivation center not subject to public health inspection that may also process common food allergens."
- Allergen labeling as specified in the *Federal Food, Drug and Cosmetics Act*[13], the *Federal Fair Packaging and Labeling Act*[14], and the *Illinois Food, Drug and Cosmetic Act*[15].
- A clearly legible warning on the front of packages indicating that they are medical cannabis infused products and not food.
- A warning that the product contains medical cannabis and is intended for consumption only by registered qualifying patients.
- Date of manufacture.
- "Use by date."
- The pre-mixed weight (in ounces or grams) of usable cannabis in the package. *Section 80(a)(3)(A-I)*.

Inventory and tracking of medical cannabis products

After a product has been packaged and labeled, it must be entered into a data collection system. *Section 105(f)*. A data collection system integrated with a cultivation center's cannabis plant monitoring system and other management systems should enable a cultivation center to track every individual product in its inventory. Being able to track individual packages facilitates the law's goal of deterring theft and diversion.

The law does not make specific rules concerning data collection systems. The Department of Agriculture and Department of Public Health may make rules in their forthcoming regulations. *Sections 165(b)(4), 165(c)(2,8)*. Tracking information could potentially be made usable to dispensaries after they receive products.

---

13. 21 U.S.C. 300.
14. 15 U.S.C. 1451.
15. 410 ILCS 620/.

Employees

Regulation of employee conduct is another way the law seeks to protect against theft and diversion. Generally, anyone who routinely performs tasks at a cultivation center or on behalf of a cultivation center and anyone who makes decisions for the cultivation center is a "cultivation center agent." *Section 10(f)*. This does not include independent contractors. The Department of Agriculture may exercise reasonable discretion to adopt additional rules of conduct for cultivation center agents. *Section 165(c)(8)*.

Pre-hire State Police background investigation

Controlling employee conduct begins with deciding who is eligible to become an agent in the first place. The law prohibits individuals who have been convicted of certain types of crimes from participating in the industry. In order to verify that a prospective board member, officer, owner, or employee has not been convicted of a prohibited offense, the law requires criminal background investigations to be performed by the Illinois State Police. Background investigations entail a state and federal criminal records check and require the submission of fingerprint samples. *Section 95(a)*.

No "excluded offenses"

Individuals who have been convicted of "excluded offenses" cannot participate in a cultivation center as a board member, officer, employee or agent of any sort. *Sections 100(f), 105(g)*.

> **Violent crime excluded offense:** The first type of excluded offense is a violent crime. This specifically means a violent crime as defined by *Section 3* of *Illinois' Rights of Crime Victims and Witnesses Act*[16]. It also includes similar violent crime felonies in another states. *Section 10(l)(1)*.

> **Controlled substance excluded offense (and waiver):** The second type of excluded offense is a felony violation

---

16. 725 ILCS 120/.

of a state or federal controlled substances law.

Section 10(l)(2). The Department of Agriculture may waive this restriction for an individual who demonstrates that the activity underlying his conviction involved facilitating a medical use of cannabis. Specifically, the Department "may waive this restriction if a person demonstrates to the registering Department's satisfaction that his or her conviction was for the possession, cultivation, transfer, or delivery of a reasonable amount of cannabis intended for medical use." *Section 10(l)(2).*

Cultivation center agent identification card

After completing the State Police background investigation, a prospective employee must apply for a "cultivation center agent identification card" through the Department of Agriculture. *Section 10(g).* The law instructs the agency to make a decision approving or denying an application within 30 days of receiving it. *Section 100(a)(1).* If approved, the agency shall then issue the agent identification card within 15 business days. *Section 100(a)(2).*

Agent identification cards contain the following information:

- Name of cardholder.
- Date of issuance.
- Date of expiration (one year after date of issuance).
- A random, unique 10-digit alphanumeric number.
- A photograph of the cardholder.
- Registry identification number of the cultivation center. *Section 100(c)(1-4).*

Rules of the agent identification card

The law requires employees to wear their agent identification cards at all times to ensure that only registered individuals have access to the cultivation center premises. The Department of Agriculture may make additional rules for cultivation center agent identification cards in its forthcoming regulations. *Section 165(c)(8).*

Visible at all times: Employees must keep their agent identification cards visible on their person at all times while on the property of a cultivation center and while transporting cannabis to a dispensary. *Section 100(b).*

Retrieve card upon employee termination:
A cultivation center must retrieve an agent identification card immediately upon the termination of the agent. *Section 100(d).*

Report lost cards: If a card becomes missing, lost, or stolen, a cultivation center agent must report it to the State Police and Department of Agriculture within 24 hours of discovering the theft or loss. *Section 100(e).*

Application and renewal fees to be determined

A prospective employee must submit an application fee to initiate the process with the Department of Agriculture. The law does not establish the amount of the fee but leaves it to the reasonable discretion of the Department of Agriculture to decide the amount in its forthcoming regulations. The agency also has authority to establish the amount of renewal fees for cultivation center agents. *Section 165(c)(9).*

PRINCIPAL
OFFICERS AND BOARD MEMBERS

The law expects a prospective cultivation center to demonstrate that it is composed of competent, qualified, and reputable personnel. Before a prospective cultivation center submits an application, all of its key individuals must undergo background investigations performed by the Illinois State Police. Individuals who have been convicted of certain types of crimes are barred from participating. *Section 85(d)(10).*

Identify key individuals and entities

Identifying key decision makers means naming not just the individuals who commit management expertise but also the corporations and other entities who may vote shares or otherwise exert ownership or control over any part the organization. There can be no secret or undisclosed owners or members. *Section 85(d)(9).*

A prospective cultivation center must disclose the names, addresses, and dates of birth of all of the following individuals:

- Principal officers.
- Board members.
- Registered agents.
- Any person having direct or indirect pecuniary interest in the cultivation center. *(Section 85(d)(9).*

Additionally, a prospective cultivation center must identify all organizations and legal entities which hold a direct or indirect pecuniary interest. This includes:

Trusts: An applicant must disclose the names and addresses of all beneficiaries of any trust that holds an interest in the prospective cultivation center.

Corporations: An applicant must disclose the names and addresses of all stockholders and directors of any corporation that holds an interest in the prospective cultivation center.

Partnerships: An applicant must disclose the names and addresses of all partners, both general and limited, of any partnership that holds an interest in the prospective cultivation center. *Section 85(d)(9).*

Must be 21 years of age or older

All principal officers, board members, and agents must be 21 years of age or older. It is grounds for denial of an application if an individual does not meet the age requirement. *Section 85(d)(3).*

State Police Background Investigations

In order to verify that a prospective principal officer, board member, or agent has not been convicted of a prohibited offense, the law requires criminal background investigations to be performed by the Illinois State Police. Background investigations entail a state and federal criminal records check and require the submission of fingerprint samples. *Section 95(a)*.

No "excluded offenses"

Individuals who have been convicted of "excluded offenses" cannot participate in a cultivation center as a board member, officer, employee, or agent of any sort. *Sections 100(f), 105(g)*.

> **No violent crimes:** No principal officer, board member, or agent may have a conviction for a violent crime. This specifically means a violent crime as defined by *Section 3* of *Illinois' Rights of Crime Victims and Witnesses Act*[17]. It also includes similar violent crime felony in another states. *Section 10(l)(1)*.

> **Controlled substance excluded offense (and waiver):** No principal officer, board member, or agent may have a conviction for a state or federal controlled substances violation. The Department of Agriculture may waive this restriction for an individual who demonstrates that the activity underlying his conviction involved facilitating a medical use of cannabis. Specifically, the Department "may waive this restriction if a person demonstrates to the registering Department's satisfaction that his or her conviction was for the possession, cultivation, transfer, or delivery of a reasonable amount of cannabis intended for medical use." *Section 10(l)(1-2)*.

No felony convictions

No person who has been convicted of a felony may participate in a cultivation center as a principal officer or board member. This means any felony whatsoever in Illinois, in any other state, or under federal law. *Section 85(e)(6)*.

17. 725 ILCS 120/.

No gambling offenses

No person who has been convicted of a gambling offense can participate in a cultivation center as principal officer or board member. This specifically means any type of gambling offense, not just a felony, under *Article 28* (gambling and related offenses) of *Illinois Criminal Code,* and it also includes similar laws of other states.

Relevant knowledge and experience

The law asks a prospective cultivation center to discuss the professional backgrounds of its principal officers, board members, and other key agents. The law specifically mentions agriculture, cultivation, and horticulture, suggesting this sort of experience may be one of the ways in which the Department of Agriculture can distinguish one particular applicant from among a pool of many others who are qualified.

The law asks members of prospective cultivation centers to provide information concerning their:

- Academic degrees. *Section 85(d)(8).*
- Certifications. *Section 85(d)(8).*
- Relevant experience with related businesses. *Section 85(d)(8).*
- "Experience with agriculture techniques and industry standards." *Section 85(d)(7).*
- "Experience with the cultivation of agricultural or horticultural products, operating an agriculturally related business, or operating a horticulture business." *Section 85(d)(13).*

Negative reporting triggers for board members

Prospective board members must disclose certain negative events that transpired at other businesses they served for as a board member. This includes any time a business they served for was ever:

- Convicted of a criminal offense.
- Fined.
- Censured.

• Involved in an administrative proceeding which resulted in the suspension or revocation of a license or registration. *Section 85(d)(4).*

None of these events disqualifies a board member, but they must be reported nonetheless.

APPLYING TO
BECOME A CULTIVATION CENTER

The law provides substantial guidance about the degree of foresight and planning a prospective cultivation center must perform ahead of filing an application to become a registered cultivation center. An applicant is required to disclose essential details about its proposed business and operating plans in order to assist the Department of Agriculture in evaluating the applicant. In addition to the requirements laid out below, the agency may compel the disclosure of further information by drafting appropriate regulations. The agency must itself review all applications to determine the qualifications and suitability of each prospective cultivation center to operate such an enterprise. The agency can award no more than one registration in each district of the Illinois State Police District.

At a minimum, the following information must be disclosed in an application:

• Proposed legal name of the cultivation center.
• Proposed physical address of the cultivation center.
• A description of the cultivation center's "enclosed locked facility."
• Name, address, and date of birth of each principal officer and board member, all of whom must be 21 years of age or older.
• Any instances in which a particular negative event transpired at a business that a board member served

for in the past (see "Negative reporting triggers for board members" above).
• Cultivation plans.
• Inventory plans.
• Packaging plans.
• Proposed operating bylaws.
• Experience with agricultural, horticultural, and cultivation techniques and industry standards.
• Any academic degrees, certifications, or relevant experience with a related business.
• Identities of all individuals and entities holding a pecuniary interest.
• Verification from Illinois State Police that all criminal background investigations of principal officers, board members, and registered agents have been conducted.
• A copy of the current local zoning ordinance and proof that a cultivation center would be in compliance.
• An application fee (the amount of which shall be determined by Department of Agriculture regulations).
• Any other information the Department of Agriculture may require in its regulations. *Section 85(d)(1-13)*.

Operating Bylaws

The law instructs a prospective cultivation center to submit "operating bylaws" as part of its application. The operating bylaws contain detailed information about the design and management procedures of a cultivation center.

Specifically, the operating bylaws consist of:

• Procedures for the oversight of the cultivation center.
• Procedures for the development and implementation of a cannabis plant monitoring system.
• Procedures for a medical cannabis container system.
• Procedures for accurate record keeping.
• A staffing plan.
• A security plan reviewed by Illinois State Police.
Section 85(d)(6).

Application Fees to be Determined

A fee must be submitted with an application for a cultivation center registration, but the law does not establish the amount of the fee. Cultivation centers who are awarded registrations are also subject to an initial registration fee, followed by renewal fees every year thereafter. The law leaves it to the Department of Agriculture to establish the amount of these fees using its reasonable discretion. *Sections 85(b-c), 165(c)(10).*

Confidentiality of application information

A cultivation center's application is confidential information, which means that the Department of Agriculture and its employees may not disclose anything contained therein. This includes everything from the identities of principal officers and board members to strategic elements of the business plan, including facility design and location, infused products plans, and more.

Specifically, the following information is confidential:

> *"Applications and renewals, their contents, and supporting information submitted by or on behalf of cultivation centers and dispensing organizations in compliance with this Act, including their physical addresses. Section 145(a)(2).*

Breach of a cultivation center's confidential information constitutes a Class B misdemeanor punishable by a fine of $1,000. *Section 145(c).*

Grounds for Denial of Application

The law instructs the Department of Agriculture that it must deny a cultivation center's application for a number of specific reasons:

- Applicant failed to submit all required materials.
- Applicant's plans do not satisfy Ag Dept.'s regulations for cultivation center oversight.
- Applicant's plans do not satisfy Ag Dept.'s security regulations.

• Applicant's plans do not satisfy Ag Dept.'s inventory regulations.
• Applicant does not satisfy Ag Dept.'s recordkeeping regulations.
• Applicant would not be in compliance with local zoning rules.
• The application contains false information.
Section 85(e)(1-2, 8).

Grounds for denial related to the prospective principal officers and board members of a cultivation center include:

• A prospective principal officer or board member has been convicted of a violent crime.
• A prospective principal officer or board member has been convicted of a controlled substances felony (and does not qualify for a medical use waiver).
• A principal officer or board member has been convicted of a felony.
A principal officer or board member has been convicted of a gambling or related offense.
• A prospective principal officer or board member has served for a cultivation center or dispensary which has had its registration revoked.
• A principal officer or board member is under the age of 21.
Section 85(e)(3-7).

Ongoing
Legal Compliance

After receiving a registration to operate, a cultivation center must maintain an ongoing relationship with the Department of Agriculture and Department of Public Health in order to ensure ongoing compliance with the law and subsequent regulations.

Reporting and Records

Accurate record-keeping is fundamental to the Department of Agriculture's ability to monitor cultivation centers to verify that no cannabis is stolen or diverted, and that a cultivation center is otherwise conducting its operations according to good practice. The law requires cultivation centers to file weekly reports with the agency as part of their ongoing compliance duties. *Section 85(d)(6)*. Forthcoming regulations will establish more precisely what kind of data the weekly reports must contain. *Section 165(c)(2)*. Likely the agency will seek data from the cannabis plant monitoring system, the medical cannabis container database, and more.

> **Inventory of cannabis plants:** The law requires cultivation centers to file weekly reports showing the inventory of all cannabis plants growing in the facility. *Section 85(d)(6)*. The law does not address specifically what other data should be included in the plant inventory report, but the Department of Agriculture's forthcoming regulations may address the point. *Section 165(c)(2)*. Given that a cultivation center is required to maintain a "cannabis plant monitoring system" capable of "documenting each cannabis plant and... monitoring plant development throughout the life cycle of a cannabis plant..." *(Section 10(c))*, it seems likely that the Department of Agriculture may request to review some of this data as part of the weekly reporting requirements.

> **Packages and containers:** Packaged buds of cannabis, packaged infused products, and packaged edible items are entered into a database for tracking purposes. *Sections 85(d)(6), 105(f)*. Such a database would have the ability to store information about every product that was ever made at a cultivation center. It is therefore likely that the Department of Agriculture will want to review this information regularly.

> **Destruction of medical cannabis:** "All cannabis byproduct, scrap, and harvested cannabis not intended for

distribution must be destroyed and disposed of pursuant to State law." A cultivation center must notify the Department of Agriculture and State Police prior to destroying cannabis, and must retain documentation related to the destruction for at least five years. *Section 180.*

Notify authorities of theft or lost product: A cultivation center must notify local law enforcement, the Illinois State Police, and the Department of Agriculture within 24 hours of discovery of any theft or loss of cannabis or cannabis products. *Section 105(J)*

Notify authorities of lost agent cards: If a cultivation center agent's identification card becomes missing, lost, or stolen, it must be reported to the State Police and Department of Agriculture within 24 hours of discovering the theft or loss. *Section 100(e).*

Random Inspections

Naturally, the agencies with enforcement duties related to cultivation centers may wish to visit the physical premises of a facility to verify firsthand that everything is in compliant order. The Department of Agriculture, the Department of Public Health, and the State Police all have power to impose random inspections on cultivation centers. *Section 105(h-i).*

Annual Renewal of cultivation center registration

Cultivation center registrations must be renewed and a renewal fee paid every year. The Department of Agriculture shall notify a cultivation center 90 days ahead of expiration that its registration renewal is coming due. If the cultivation center's registration has not been suspended or revoked, and if the cultivation center submits a renewal application and fee within the first 45 day, then the renewal shall be granted. The law does not specify what may happen if the cultivation center does not submit the renewal application within the first 45 days. *Section 90.*

7% cultivation privilege tax

Sections 190 - 215 of the new law compose what is called the *Medical Cannabis Cultivation Privilege Tax Law*, which imposes a tax on cultivation centers "for the privilege of cultivating medical cannabis." The rate of the tax is "7% of the sales price per ounce." This tax is "in addition to all other occupation or privilege taxes imposed by the State of Illinois or by any municipal corporation or political subdivision thereof." *Section 200(a-b).* The tax accrues monthly and comes due for payment on the 20th of each month. *Section 210.*

Political contributions prohibited

By way of amending Illinois' *Election Code*[18], the law prohibits cultivation centers and dispensaries (and political action committees created by them) from contributing payments to political campaigns. *Section 900.*

Immunities for cultivation centers and employees

The law gives explicit assurances to cultivation centers that they enjoy immunity from prosecution, arrest, and other penalties under State law for engaging in activities related to medical cannabis production in the manner prescribed by law. *Section 25(g-h).*

Suspension and revocation of registration

The Department of Agriculture may punish a cultivation center for violating the *Compassionate Use of Medical Cannabis Pilot Program Act* by suspending or revoking the cultivation center's registration. A suspension or revocation is considered a final agency action, which means a cultivation center does not have a right to an appeal or to otherwise object within the agency. The appropriate venue for raising an objection is the local Circuit Court. *Section 110(a-b).*

---

18. 10 ILCS 5/9-45.

DISPENSARIES

Subjects Covered:

- Functions of a dispensary

- 60 dispensaries, reasonably dispersed

- Market constraints

- Location restrictions

- Security

- Products and services for sale

- Interacting with patients and caregivers

- Employees

- Principal officers and board members

- Applying to become a dispensary

- Ongoing legal compliance

When cannabis or cannabis products leave a cultivation center, their only legal destination is a dispensary, which is the other new type of business created by the *Compassionate Use of Medical Cannabis Pilot Program Act*. Dispensaries are like retail stores or pharmacies where registered patients and caregivers can browse and purchase cannabis products. But a dispensary is very different from any other sort of retail store or pharmacy because of special issues involving interactions with patients.

As patients' only point of contact to the medical cannabis industry, dispensaries bear responsibility for verifying that customers are legitimately registered as a patient or caregiver before every transaction. Dispensaries also perform a vital role in helping patients understand which particular varieties of cannabis or methods of consumption are most appropriate for each patient's unique medical condition, tastes, and preferences.

Functions
of a Dispensary

The basic purpose of a dispensary is simple: sell medical cannabis products. But medical cannabis happens to be a very closely regulated product, which means there are layers of procedures that must be followed in order to ensure that every unit is distributed only to legitimate cardholders.

Verifying cardholders

Before every transaction, dispensaries must verify that a customer is a registered patient or caregiver. The law establishes a system of procedures for checking a cardholder's information against the Department of Public Health's cardholder registry database. *Section 130(i).*

Selling products

In its simplest sense, a dispensary is a retail store, but its products are exclusive and tightly regulated. Like any store, a dispensary should conform to basic good management and customer service practices. This includes keeping good inventory and records, planning appropriate purchases from cultivation centers, accommodating patients, and otherwise conducting the business of selling products.

Providing information about cannabis treatment

As the only point of contact for cardholders to the medical cannabis industry, dispensaries perform a vital role in educating patients about the many various options for treating a condition with cannabis products. The ultimate goal is to help each patient obtain medicine that is a good fit for his medical condition and suitable to his personal tastes and preferences.

Protecting confidential information

When receiving cardholders and discussing medical cannabis treatment with them, a dispensary employee may learn private, sensitive information about a patient. The law wants to encourage free and honest dialogue between cardholders and dispensaries so that patients feel comfortable discussing their conditions and thereby gain assistance in making informed decisions about which cannabis products to purchase. The law therefore requires that information be kept confidentially and creates a legal privilege regarding patients' relationship with dispensary employees. *Section 130(j-k).*

Fundamental rules for dispensaries

The following rules apply to dispensaries:

No use or consumption on property: A dispensary may not assist a patient in administering cannabis or allow a patient to sample cannabis products on the premises. *Section 130(l).*

Obtain cannabis only from IL cultivation centers: A dispensary may obtain cannabis and cannabis products only from cultivation centers registered under Illinois law. A dispensary may not deal in cannabis that was grown out of state or procured from an unregistered source. *Section 130(e).*

Sell only to registered patients or caregivers: A dispensary may dispense cannabis only for the purpose of assisting registered patients or their caregivers. *Section 130(f).*

60 DISPENSARIES, REASONABLY DISPERSED

The law instructs the Department of Financial and Professional Regulations to grant the rights to operate a dispensary to up to 60 organizations throughout the state.

Specifically, dispensaries should be:

> "...geographically dispersed throughout the state to allow
> all registered qualifying patients reasonable proximity
> and access to a dispensary." Section 155(a).

Deciding what is "reasonable" is in the discretion of the Department of Financial and Professional Regulation. The agency is encouraged to grant all 60 registrations. The agency may not refuse to grant a registration if there is a qualified applicant. Generally, an applicant would be qualified if it meets the minimum requirements found the in the law and DFPR's forthcoming regulations. *Section 155(a).*

It is anticipated that many prospective dispensaries may be interested in applying for a registration initially. If less than 60 apply before the initial deadline, then all may be automatic winners if all are qualified. But if there are more than 60 who apply before the initial deadline, then the Department of Financial and Professional Regulation may have to choose from among the qualified competitors by using the reasonable dispersement requirement.

MARKET CONSTRAINTS

A prospective dispensary might ponder some things about the size of the market and location of customers when calculating its potential product turnover. For example, the market is constrained by the rule that products can be used only by qualified patients with debilitating medical conditions. Furthermore, a registered cardholder receives permission to purchase cannabis at only one designated dispensary. This means the other 59 or so dispensaries can do little to compete for a patient's business if the patient has already been designated elsewhere. It also means patients may tend to default to the dispensary located nearest to home.

Certified patients are the only legal consumers

The potential size of the market for medical cannabis is highly restricted. Cannabis products may be used only by patients who have first been certified by a licensed physician as having a debilitating medical condition and then have been approved by the Department of Public Health's application process. *Section 130(i)*.

Patient purchase limit is 2.5 ounces per 14 days

Another control on the potential demand for medical cannabis is the restriction that a patient can buy no more than 2.5 ounces of cannabis (or the pre-mixed weight of cannabis) per two-week period. *Section 130(h)*.

Patient authorized to buy at one dispensary only

When a patient applies for a registry identification card, he must designate one and only one dispensary where he will be allowed to purchase medical cannabis products. *Section 55(a)(7)*. This decision may often boil down to a matter of nearness to home for the patient.

Sales of other products and services?

The law makes no rules authorizing or prohibiting the sale of goods and services beyond cannabis, cannabis products, and paraphernalia. The Department of Financial and Professional Regulation may use reasonable discretion to make additional rules deciding what other particular items dispensaries may sell. *Section 165(d)*. For example, DFPR may decide to adopt regulations concerning whether dispensaries are allowed to sell branded merchandise or health and wellness services.

LOCATION RESTRICTIONS

The law imposes restrictions to keep dispensaries outside of residential zones and away from schools and child care, though not as far away as cultivation centers are required to be. The powers of local governments and the attitudes of local communities are also highly relevant considerations for prospective dispensaries pondering the location of their facilities.

The following rules are explicit in the law:

Not in a residential zone: A dispensary cannot be located in an area zoned for residential use.

Away from schools (1,000 feet): A dispensary cannot be located within 1,000 feet of a pre-existing public or private:

- preschool.
- elementary school.
- secondary school.

Away from child care (1,000 feet): A dispensary cannot be located within 1,000 feet of a pre-existing:

- day care center.
- day care home.
- group day care home.
- part day child care facility.

Not in a dwelling: A dispensary cannot be located in:

- a house
- an apartment
- a condominium. *Section 130(d) for all.*

May not share space with a physician: As part of its conflicts of interests rules for the medical profession, the law prohibits a dispensary from sharing office space with a physician and also from referring patients to a physician. *Section 130(m).*

Compliance with local zoning code and other ordinances

The attitudes of the local community should be highly relevant considerations for a dispensary. County, city, and village governments possess powers which they may use in friendly or unfriendly ways relative to a prospective dispensary and its competitors. Local government's most relevant power is the power to enact ordinances for land use and development, which includes zoning and rezoning. In some circumstances, local government may be able to adjust its zoning map to either prohibit or enable a type of business like a dispensary. Local government may not, however, exercise power in a way that is inconsistent with the *Compassionate Use of Medical Cannabis Pilot Program Act. Section 140.*

A prospective dispensary must decide upon its location by the time it submits an application to become a dispensary to the Department of Financial and Professional Regulation. Along with its application, a prospective cultivation center must include a copy of the current local zoning ordinance for the area it wishes to occupy and otherwise verify that a it would be in compliance with zoning rules. *Section 85(d)(11).*

SECURITY

Naturally, the design of a dispensary must implement robust security measures because of the large amounts of cash, cannabis, and cannabis products that are on hand.

DFPR to draft security rules

Compared to cultivation centers, the law provides fewer specifications about the security requirements of dispensaries. The General Assembly has chosen instead to delegate authority to the Department of Financial and Professional Regulation to adopt appropriate rules for dispensaries' security. *Sections 130(c), 165(d).*

Restricted access to area where cannabis stored

One thing the law makes unmistakably clear about dispensary

security requirements is that the area where cannabis is stored must be locked and separated from the storefront part of the dispensary where cardholders can browse and purchase cannabis products. *Section 130(g)*.

The area where cannabis is stored must be accessible only to authorized personnel, which includes:

• Dispensary agents and employees.
• Inspectors of the Department of Financial and Professional Regulation.
• Law enforcement and other emergency personnel.
• Contractors working on jobs unrelated to medical cannabis, such as installing security devices or performing electrical wiring. *Section 130(g)*.

Alarm system

The Department of Financial and Professional Regulation's security requirements for dispensaries must include "a fully operational security alarm system." *Section 165(d)(4)*.

Unloading cannabis arriving from a cultivation center

Given the volume and value of cannabis that will be involved in deliveries, the safe and secure transportation of cannabis from a cultivation center to a dispensary is essential to a healthy medical cannabis industry. The law does not decide any rules related to the transportation of cannabis products, but it recognizes the importance of such rules. The law specifically delegates authority to the Department of Agriculture to adopt rules for safe transportation. *Section 165(c)(6)*. Additionally the Department of Financial and Professional Regulation may also exercise discretion to adopt rules covering the unloading of cannabis after a shipment arrives at a dispensary. *Section 165(d)(4)*.

Employee Management

Oversight of employees is a critical part of preventing theft and diversion. Prospective employees of a dispensary must undergo background investigations performed by the Illinois State Police before beginning work. Then once employed, employees must wear identification cards and adhere to rules governing the use of the cards. *Section 120.*

Recordkeeping

A dispensary is required to keep meticulous records of its sales as part of its ongoing legal compliance requirements. *Section 130(b,j).* Keeping good records generally helps the Department of Financial and Professional Regulation verify that no cannabis has been stolen or diverted.

PRODUCTS
AND SERVICES FOR SALE

A dispensary is the only type of business in Illinois that may sell the buds of cannabis plants, cannabis infused medicine, and edible foods produced at an Illinois cultivation center. The law requires dispensaries to keep track of the weight of cannabis (or the pre-mixed weight of cannabis used to make a product) involved in every transaction with a cardholder. This is a way to ensure that no cardholder exceeds the legal "adequate supply."

But beyond items which originate at a cultivation center, the law does not make many rules regarding what other sorts of products and services a dispensary may sell. If it wishes, the Department of Financial and Professional Regulation might exercise reasonable discretion to authorize or restrict the sale of other items. One compelling reason to do so would be to maintain the law's insistence on purely medical attitudes about cannabis, at least during the pilot program period. The sale of items which might tend to suggest or promote non-medical ideas about cannabis, for example, could be made subject to restriction.

Patient's "Adequate Supply"

A dispensary may sell up to 2.5 ounces of cannabis but no more to a patient or the patient's caregiver during a 14-day period. *Section 130(h)*. Dispensaries are required to keep record of patients' purchases in order to prevent them from exceeding their adequate supply. *Section 130(j)*. If infused products or baked goods are among a patient's purchases, then a dispensary must record the pre-mixed weight of the cannabis used to make the products. *Section 10(a)(4)*.

Cannabis buds may be sold

A dispensary may sell buds of cannabis plants procured from a registered Illinois cultivation center. *Section 105(f)*. Cannabis buds may be preferred by patients who smoke or vaporize the buds, or else use them to make their own edible baked goods at home.

Saplings of cannabis plants may not be sold

Illinois dispensaries may not sell live young saplings of cannabis plants to cardholders to take home and continue growing. A cultivation center is only place in Illinois where cannabis plants can legally grow. *Section 10(e)*.

Edibles and infused products may be sold

A dispensary may sell baked food items such as brownies and cookies as well as cannabis infused medicine products such as pills, ointments, serums, lozenges, etc. These items must be manufactured at an Illinois cultivation center and packaged with legally compliant labels. *Section 80(a)*. If a dispensary sells edible cannabis products, then it must display a placard which states, "Edible cannabis infused products were produced in a kitchen not subject to public health inspections that may also process common food allergens." *Section 80(a)(4)*.

Paraphernalia may be sold

The law envisions dispensaries selling "paraphernalia" to patients. This is implied by *Section 25(f)(1)*, which creates an immunity for dispensary employees who sell paraphernalia to cardholders. The law does not define paraphernalia, but generally the term includes glass and metal pipes, vaporizers, cigarette rolling papers, etc. The Department of Financial and Professional Regulation may decide to adopt rules governing the sale of various types of paraphernalia. *Section 165(d)*.

Branded merchandise undecided

Some producers and distributors of cannabis products and paraphernalia in other states sell merchandise branded with images that portray cannabis as cool or recreational. Some dispensaries in other states carry the branded merchandise of these companies, such as T-shirt, hats, and stickers. The *Compassionate Use of Medical Cannabis Pilot Program Act* makes no rules prohibiting or enabling the sale of branded merchandise, but generally the law wants to promote a sterile, strictly medicinal attitude about marijuana. Therefore, if the Department of Financial and Professional Regulation desired, it may be able to adopt reasonable regulations to prohibit dispensaries from selling items which are inconsistent with the spirit of the law. *Section 165(d)*.

Healing services and wellness classes undecided

Some dispensaries in other states offer health and wellness services to patients, such acupuncture, massage, and yoga classes for example. Illinois' law does not address whether dispensaries may offer health-related services, but it may be within the scope of the Department of Financial and Professional Regulation's reasonable discretion to adopt appropriate regulations. *Section 165(d)*.

INTERACTING WITH PATIENTS AND CAREGIVERS

To ensure cannabis is obtainable only by properly registered cardholders, dispensaries must verify their customers' details before every transaction. Dispensaries must also keep information about their customers in confidence, in order to encourage patients to discuss their medical conditions openly and honestly.

Verifying cardholders

The law establishes a system of procedures for checking a cardholder's information against the Department of Public Health's verification system. *Section 130(i)*. A "cardholder" is either a patient or a caregiver. *Section 109(d)*. Some patients may be so disabled that it would not be reasonable for them to visit a dispensary. The law therefore allows patients to designate a "caregiver" who receives authority to obtain medical cannabis from a dispensary on behalf of the patient. *Section 10(i)*. Caregivers and patients are both registered into the same verification system managed by the Department of Public Health. *Section 150*. Before dispensing cannabis, a dispensary must verify a customer's information against the verification system to ensure the customer is presenting true and accurate information.

A dispensary must verify the following before every transaction:

1. That the card is valid.

2. That the person presenting the card is truly the person to whom the card is registered.

3. That this dispensary is the properly designated dispensary for this cardholder.

4. That the patient has not exceeded his adequate supply of 2.5 ounces per 14-day period. *Section 130(i)(1-4)*.

Informing patients about medical cannabis options

An important function of a dispensary is helping patients select appropriate cannabis products to treat their conditions and accommodate their unique preferences. Some patients, for example, may benefit more from ingesting an infused product or baked item as opposed to smoking or vaporizing cannabis. It is important that patients receive accurate information about cannabis products so that they can make informed decisions about their treatment options. The law therefore wants patients to feel comfortable talking honestly with dispensary employees, and it tries to accomplish this goal by requiring dispensaries to maintain information in confidence. Section 130(j).

Beyond insisting on confidentiality, the law makes few rules to guide dispensaries in their relations with customers. The Department of Financial and Professional Regulation may decide to use reasonable discretion to adopt appropriate regulations. *Section 165(d)*. For example, the agency might advise dispensary employees to follow particular guidelines in their conversations with patients and caregivers. Another possible avenue could be requiring dispensary employees who interact with patients and caregivers to receive some sort of training, or else require them to have a background in a relevant field, such as pharmacy or social work.

Confidentiality of patient information

Dispensaries are required to maintain internal records of all sales transactions, indicating the date and time of each sale and whether the sale was dispensed to the patient or to the designated caregiver. *Section 130(j)*. Records must indicate the weight of cannabis involved in each transaction to help ensure that no patient exceeds the legally allotted adequate supply of 2.5 ounces per 14-day period. These records must remain confidential. *Section 145(a)(4)*. Generally this means employees should refrain from repeating anything a patient says about himself or his medical condition to anyone besides another employee of the dispensary. The penalty for a dispensary or employee who breaches the confidentiality of a cardholder's information is a Class B misdemeanor with a $1,000 fine. *Section 145(c)*.

Legal privilege created

The law extends the physician-patient privilege[19] to cover a patient's relationship with dispensary employees. A patient possessing a legal privilege can prevent dispensary employees from testifying under oath about communications that transpired between them. This particular privilege covers "communications and records concerning qualifying patients' debilitating condition." *Section 130(k)*. The privilege is part of the law's effort to encourage open and honest communication between patients and dispensaries so that patients can make informed decisions about treatment options.

19. The parameters of the physician-patient privilege are found in *Section 8-802* of Illinois' *Code of Civil Procedure*.

No sampling or assisting

A dispensary may not permit any person to consume cannabis on its property. This means a dispensary cannot allow a patient to sample a product or give a demonstration of how a product should be smoked, vaporized, ingested, or otherwise administered. *Section 130(l).*

Display placard if selling infused products

If a dispensary sells edible cannabis products, it must display a placard which states:

> *"Edible cannabis infused products were produced in a kitchen not subject to public health inspections that may also process common food allergens." Section 80(a)(4).*

EMPLOYEES

Controlling employees' conduct is one of the law's ways of protecting against theft and diversion. Prospective employees must undergo a background investigation performed by the Illinois State Police before they may begin work at a dispensary. Then after an employee has been hired, he must wear a "dispensing organization agent identification card" at all times on the premises and follow other general rules of conduct related to the card. *Section 120.*

Generally, anyone who routinely performs tasks at a dispensary or on behalf of a dispensary and anyone who makes decisions for the dispensary is a "medical cannabis dispensing organization agent," defined as "a principal officer, board member, employee, or agent of a registered dispensary who is 21 years of age or older and has not been convicted of an excluded offense." This does not include independent contractors. *Section 10(o).* The Department of Financial and Professional Regulation may exercise reasonable discretion to adopt additional rules of conduct for dispensary agents. *Section 165(d).*

Pre-hire State Police background investigation

Controlling employee conduct begins with deciding who is eligible to become an agent in the first place. The law prohibits individuals who have been convicted of certain types of crimes from participating in the medical cannabis industry. In order to verify that a prospective board member, officer, or employee has not been convicted of a prohibited offense, the law requires criminal background investigations to be performed by the Illinois State Police. Background investigations entail a state and federal criminal records check and require the submission of fingerprint samples. *Section 115(d)*.

No "excluded offenses"

Individuals who have been convicted of "excluded offenses" cannot participate in a dispensary as a board member, officer, employee, or any other sort of agent. *Section 120(f)*.

> **Violent crime excluded offense:** The first type of excluded offense is a violent crime. This specifically means a violent crime as defined by *Section 3* of *Illinois' Rights of Crime Victims and Witnesses Act*[20]. It also includes a similar violent crime felony in any other state. *Section 10(l)(1)*.

> **Controlled substance excluded offense (and waiver):** The second type of excluded offense is a felony violation of a state or federal controlled substances law. The law gives authority to the Department of Financial and Professional Regulation to waive the restriction on controlled substance convictions if an individual can demonstrate that his activity underlying a conviction involved facilitating a legitimate medical use of cannabis. Specifically, the agency "may waive this restriction if the person demonstrates to the registering Department's satisfaction that his or her conviction was for the possession, cultivation, transfer, or delivery of a reasonable amount of cannabis intended for medical use." *Section 10(l)(2)*.

---

20. 725 ILCS 120/.

Dispensing organization agent identification card

After completing the State Police background check, a prospective employee must apply for a "dispensing organization agent identification card" through the Department of Financial and Professional Regulation. *Section 10(j).* The law instructs the agency to make a decision approving or denying an application within 30 days. If approved, the Department of Agriculture shall then issue the agent identification card within 15 business days. *Section 120(a)(1-2).*

Agent identification cards contain the following information:

- Name of cardholder.
- Date of issuance.
- Date of expiration.
- A random, unique 10-digit alphanumeric number.
- A photograph of the cardholder. *Section 120(c)(1-4).*

Rules of the agent identification card

The law requires employees to wear their agent identification cards at all times on the premises of a dispensary but makes few other rules regarding employee conduct. The Department of Financial and Professional Regulation may adopt rules in its forthcoming regulations. *Section 165(d).*

Visible at all times: Employees must keep their agent identification cards visible on their person at all times while on the property of a dispensary. *Section 120(b).*

Retrieve card upon employee termination: A dispensary must retrieve an agent's identification card immediately upon termination of the agent. *Section 120(d)[21].*

---

21. *Section 120(d)* actually states that dispensary agent identification cards must be returned to the *cultivation center* upon termination of the employee, but this is obviously an error.

Report lost cards: If a card becomes missing, lost, or stolen, a dispensary agent must report it to the State Police and Department of Agriculture[22] within 24 hours of discovering the theft or loss. *Section 120(e).*

Application fees to be determined

A prospective employee must submit an application fee to initiate the process with the Department of Financial and Professional Regulation. The law does not establish the amount of the fee but leaves it to the reasonable discretion of the agency to decide the amount in its forthcoming regulations. The agency also has authority to establish the amount of renewal fees for dispensary agents. *Section 165(d)(1).*

Promise not to divert cannabis

A dispensary's principal officers, board members, and agents must submit signed statements to the Department of Financial and Professional Regulation "stating that they will not divert medical cannabis." *Section 115(c)(7).*

"Agent-in-charge"

The law instructs the Department of Financial and Professional Regulation that its forthcoming regulations should make rules relating to "agent-in-charge oversight requirements." *Section 165(d)(2).* But the law gives no further guidance about what it envisions as the agent-in-charge's special duties relative to other agents.

PRINCIPAL OFFICERS
AND BOARD MEMBERS

The law expects a prospective dispensary to demonstrate that it is composed of competent, qualified, and reputable personnel. Before

22. *Section 120(e)* states that dispensary agents must report lost cards to the Department of Agriculture rather than to the Department of Financial and Professional Regulation, but this may be an error.

a prospective dispensary submits an application, all of its principal officers and board members must undergo background investigations performed by the Illinois State Police. Individuals who have been convicted of certain types of crimes are barred from participating.

Although the law requires a prospective cultivation center to disclose information about all individuals, organizations, and entities who hold a "direct or indirect pecuniary interest" in the venture *(Section 85(d)(9))*, no such requirement is imposed on prospective dispensaries. The law asks only that dispensaries identify their principal officers and board members. *Section 115(c)(4).*

Must be 21 years of age or older

All officers, board members, and agents of a dispensary must 21 years of age or older. It is grounds for denial of an application if a member does not meet the age requirement. *Section 115(c)(4).*

State Police Background Investigations

The law requires all principal officers and board members to undergo a criminal background investigation performed by the Illinois State Police. Background investigations entail a state and federal criminal records check and require the submission of fingerprint samples. Individuals convicted of certain types of crimes are prohibited from participating in a dispensary as an officer, board member, or employee. *Section 115(d).*

> **No violent crime convictions:** Individuals who have been convicted of a violent crime cannot participate in a dispensary. *Section 115(f)(4).* This specifically means a violent crime defined in *Section 3* of *Illinois' Rights of Crime Victims and Witnesses Act[23]*, and also includes violent crime felonies in other states. *Section 10(l)(1).*

> **No Controlled substance convictions (and waiver):** No one who has been convicted of a controlled substance violation can participate in a dispensary as a principal officer or board member. The Department of Financial and Professional Regulation may waive this restriction for an individual who demonstrates that the activity underlying

23. 725 ILCS 120/.

the conviction involved facilitating a medical use of cannabis. Specifically, the agency "may waive this restriction if the person demonstrates to the registering Department's satisfaction that his or her conviction was for the possession, cultivation, transfer, or delivery of a reasonable amount of cannabis intended for medical use." *Section 10(l)(2).*

Although the law prohibits anyone who has ever been convicted of a felony or a gambling offense from being a principal officer or board member of a cultivation center *(Section 85(e)(6-7)*, it does prohibit such persons from being a principal officer or board member of a dispensary.

Negative reporting triggers for board members

Prospective board members of a dispensary must disclose certain negative events that transpired at other businesses they served for as a board member. Specifically, board members must disclose:

> *"Information, in writing, regarding any instances in which a business or not-for-profit that any of the prospective board members managed or served on the board was convicted, or had a registration suspended or revoked in any administrative or judicial proceeding. Section 115(c)(5).*

Officers and board members cannot be cardholders

A person who is a registered patient or caregiver may not also be a principal officer or board member of a dispensary. *Section 115(f)(7).*

Promise not to divert cannabis

A dispensary's principal officers, board members, and agents must submit signed statements to the Department of Financial and Professional Regulation "stating that they will not divert medical cannabis." *Section 115(c)(7).*

Applying
to Become a Dispensary

The law provides substantial guidance about the degree of foresight and planning a prospective dispensary must perform ahead of filing an application to become a registered dispensary. An applicant must disclose essential details about its proposed business and operating plans in order to assist the Department of Financial and Professional Regulation in evaluating the applicant. In addition to the requirements laid out below, the agency may compel the disclosure of further information by drafting appropriate regulations. The agency must itself review all applications to determine the qualifications and suitability of each prospective dispensary to operate such a business. The agency may award up to 60 registrations, and must try to disperse them throughout the state so that "all registered qualifying patients [have] reasonable proximity and access to a dispensing organization." *Section 155(a).*

At a minimum, the following information must be disclosed in an application:

> • A non-refundable application fee in an amount to be established by DFPR regulations.
> • The proposed legal name of the dispensary.
> • The proposed physical address of the dispensary.
> • The name, address, and date of birth of each principal officer and board member, all of whom must be 21 years of age or older.
> • Any instance in which a particular negative event transpired at an organization that a board member previously served for." (see "Negative reporting triggers for board members" above).
> • Proposed operating bylaws.
> • Signed statements from every agent stating they will not divert medical cannabis. *Section 115(c)(1-7).*

Operating By-laws

The law instructs a prospective dispensary to include its proposed operating bylaws in its application. The operating bylaws include:

- Procedures for the oversight of the dispensary.
- Procedures to ensure accurate recordkeeping.
- Security measures in compliance with DFPR's forthcoming regulations.
- A description of the enclosed, locked facility where medical cannabis will be stored. *Section 115(c)(6).*

Application Fees to be Determined

A fee must be submitted with an application for a dispensary registration, but the law does not establish the amount of the fee. Dispensaries who are awarded registrations are also subject to an initial registration fee, followed by renewal fees every year thereafter. The law leaves it to the Department of Financial and Professional Regulation to establish the amount of these fees using its reasonable discretion. *Sections 115(c)(1), 165(d)(1).*

Confidentiality of application information

A dispensary's application is confidential information, which means that the Department of Financial and Professional Regulation and its employees generally may not disclose anything contained in an application outside of the agency. This information may be shared outside the agency only with the State Police or other agencies with authority under the law, and only for a legitimate reason. *Section 145(a).* Protected information in an application includes everything from the identities of principal officers and board members to strategic elements of the dispensary's business plan and its site location.

Specifically, the following information is confidential:

> *"Applications and renewals, their contents, and supporting information submitted by or on behalf of cultivation centers and dispensing organizations in compliance with this Act, including their physical addresses. Section 145(a)(2).*

Breach of a dispensary's confidential information constitutes a Class B misdemeanor punishable by a fine of $1,000. *Section 145(c)*.

Grounds for Denial

The law instructs the Department of Financial and Professional Regulation that it must deny an application for a number of specific reasons:

- Applicant failed to submit all required materials.
- Applicant's plans do not satisfy DFPR's security regulations.
- Applicant's plans do not satisfy DFPR's regulation for dispensary oversight.
- Applicant's plans do not satisfy DFPR's regulations for recordkeeping.
- Applicant would not be in compliance with local zoning rules. *Section 115(f)(1-3)*.

Grounds for denial related to prospective principal officers and board members of a dispensary include:

- A prospective principal officer or board member has been convicted of a violent crime.
- A prospective principal officer or board member has been convicted of a controlled substances felony (and does not qualify for a medical use waiver).
- A prospective principal officer or board member has served for a dispensary which has had its license revoked.
- A prospective principal officer or board member is under the age of 21.
- A principal officer or board member is a registered patient or caregiver. *Section (115(f)(4-7)*.

Ongoing
Legal Compliance

After receiving a registration to operate, a dispensary must maintain an ongoing relationship with the Department of Financial and Professional Regulation in order to ensure compliance with the law and subsequent regulations.

Reporting and records

Accurate recordkeeping is fundamental to the Department of Financial and Professional Regulation's ability to monitor dispensaries to verify that no cannabis is stolen or diverted, and that a dispensary is otherwise operating according to good practice.

The law requires dispensaries to maintain:

> *"internal, confidential records that include records specifying how much medical cannabis is dispensed to the registered qualifying paient and whether it was dispensed directly to the registered qualifying patient or to the designated caregiver. Each entry must include the date and time the cannabis was dispensed." Section 130(j).*

The Department of Financial and Professional Regulation is likely to review this information regularly. The law also gives the agency authority to impose additional reporting requirements as necessary. *Section 130(j).* For example, if the agency also wanted to monitor all of a dispensary's purchases from cultivation centers, then it may be able to.

Destruction of medical cannabis

If a dispensary must destroy or otherwise dispose of cannabis products other than by sale to a registered cardholder, it must notify the State Police and Department of Financial and Professional Regulation. Records related to any such destruction or disposal must be kept for at least five years. *Section 180(a,d,e).* Specifically:

"A dispensary organization shall destroy all cannabis, including cannabis-infused products, that are not sold to registered qualifying patients. Documentation of destruction and disposal shall be retained at the dispensary organization for a period of not less than 5 years." Section 180(d).

Notify authorities of lost agent identification cards

If a dispensary employee's agent identification card becomes missing, lost or stolen, it must be reported to the State Police and Department of Financial and Professional Regulation within 24 hours of discovering the theft or loss. *Section 120(e).*

Random inspections

Proper oversight entails visiting the physical premises of a dispensary on occasion to very firsthand that everything is in compliant order. The Department of Financial and Professional Regulation and the State Police both have power to impose random inspections on dispensaries. *Section 130(o).*

Annual renewal of dispensary registration

A dispensay's registration must be renewed and a renewal fee must be paid every year. The Department of Financial and Professional Regulation shall notify a dispensary 90 days ahead of expiration that its registration is coming due. If the dispensary's registration has not been suspended or revoked, and if the dispensary submits a renewal application and fee within the first 45 days, then the renewal shall be granted. The law does not specify what may happen if the dispensary does not submit the renewal application within the first 45 days. *Section 125.*

No tax for handling cannabis

Sections 190 - 215 of the law compose what is called the *Medical Cannabis Cultivation Privilege Tax Law*, which imposes the entire tax burden for the medical cannabis industry on its cultivation centers. Cultivation centers are taxed at a rate of 7% of their sales. Dispensaries are not taxed at all. But of course dispensaries are the only purchasers of cultivation centers' products, so they may indirectly share a portion of the tax burden through increased prices.

Political contributions prohibited

By way of amending Illinois' *Election Code*[24], the law prohibits cultivation centers and dispensaries (and political action committees created by them) from contributing payments to political campaigns. *Section 900.*

Immunities for dispensaries and employees

The law gives explicit assurances to dispensaries and their employees that they enjoy immunity from prosecution, arrest, and other penalties under State law for engaging in activities related to dispensing medical cannabis in the manner authorized by law. *Section 25(i)(j).*

Suspension and revocation of registration

The Department of Financial and Professional Regulation may punish a dispensary for violating the Compassionate Use of Medical Cannabis Pilot Program Act by suspending or revoking the dispensary's registration. A suspension or revocation is considered a final agency action, which means a dispensary does not have a right to an appeal or to otherwise object to the agency's decision. The appropriate venue for raising an objection is the local Circuit Court. *Section 15(e).*

The agency also has the ability to issue fines of up to $10,000 to a dispensary or one its agents. The law instructs the agency to adopted rules governing the procedure for sanctioning a dispensary and its agents. *Section 130(n).*

---

24. 10 ILCS 5/9-45.

PHYSICIANS AND HEALTH CARE

Subjects Covered:

- Physician requirements

- "Debilitating medical conditions"

- Physician's written certification

- Physician's standard of conduct

- Legal immunities

- Physician's conflict of interest rules

- Cannabis use at health care facilities

The *Compassionate Use of Medical Cannabis Pilot Program Act* wants to make sure it's still business as usual as far as health care professionals are concerned. The law is careful to create no new legal hazards or other difficulties. A licensed physician's certification of a debilitating medical condition is a prerequisite to obtaining a patient's registry identification card, which makes physicians the one and only gateway to legal medical cannabis in Illinois, just as they are with pharmaceutical drugs. If any physicians are leery of the sudden change in the legal status of cannabis, the law responds by giving explicit assurances that they are free to recommend cannabis to patients without fear of professional or legal penalty.

Registered patients are authorized to use medical cannabis at health care facilities, but smoking it is explicitly prohibited. Also, to ensure the integrity of the medical profession, the law imposes a series of conflicts of interest rules which prohibit physicians who recommend medical cannabis from participating in the industry or otherwise receiving incentives.

PHYSICIAN REQUIREMENTS

The law takes care not to enable the emergence of new non-physician service providers who might rubberstamp every patient they see with a debilitating medical condition. Only physicians who are licensed under Illinois' *Medical Practice Act*[25] and *Controlled Substances Act*[26] may certify cannabis use for a patient. The status of the physician's licenses must be in good standing. *Section 35(a)(1).*

Licensed under Illinois Medical Practice Act

To certify cannabis use for patients with debilitating medical conditions, a physician must be

> " *a doctor of medicine or doctor of osteopathy licensed under the [Illinois] Medical Practice Act." Section 35(a)(1).*

The law explicitly does not allow dentists or any other professionals to certify patients with debilitating medical conditions:

> *"It does not [authorize] a licensed practitioner under any other Act, including but no limited to the Illinois Dental Practice Act*[27]*." Section 10(s)*

Licensed under Illinois Controlled Substances Act

A physician must also hold a controlled substances license under *Article III* of the *Illinois Controlled Substances Act* in order to certify cannabis use for patients with debilitating condition. *35(a)(1)*

---

25. 225 ILCS 60/.
26. 720 ILCS 570/.
27. 225 ILCS 25/.

DEBILITATING
MEDICAL CONDITIONS

Only patients who suffer from what the law calls "debilitating medical conditions" may become authorized to use medical cannabis. *Section 10(t).*

The full list of debilitating medical conditions appears on page 1 of this book.

Generally these are conditions for which the benefits of cannabis are well demonstrated by medical science.

The Department of Public Health has power to expand the list of debilitating medical conditions so that more patients may qualify to obtain medical cannabis. Any Illinois citizen may initiate the process by filing a petition requesting that the agency consider expanding the list. The petition must identify the particular condition that the patient would like to see added to the list. The agency must acknowledge and consider the petition through a formal procedure requiring public notice and hearing. The law instructs the Department of Public Health that it must approve or deny a petition within 180 days. *Section 45.*

PHYSICIAN'S
WRITTEN CERTIFICATION

Although a previously banned substance suddenly becomes available for treating patients, the law does not intend to have a dramatic effect on the dynamics of the medical profession. The practice of diagnosing conditions and prescribing medicine remains much the same, but with a little more paperwork.

When a physician encounters a patient with a debilitating medical condition and wishes to prescribe cannabis, the proper procedure is to issue a "written certification." *Section 35(a).* Physicians are free to use their own sound professional judgment in deciding to prescribe cannabis or not to a patient who has a debilitating medical condition, just like it were any other pharmaceutical option.

Form of physician's written certification

Certifications must appear on an official form issued by the Department of Public Health. *Section 55(a)(1)*.

Physician asserts three statements

When a physician writes a certification for a patient with a debilitating medical condition, the physician asserts three statements:

> **1. Patient is likely to benefit from cannabis:** *"...that in the physician's professional opinion the patient is likely to receive therapeutic or palliative benefit from the medical use of cannabis to treat or alleviate the patient's debilitating condition or symptoms associated with the debilitating medical condition."*

> **2. Patient has a specific debilitating condition:** *"... that the qualifying patient has a debilitating medical condition and specifying the debilitating medical condition the patient has."*

> **3. Physician-patient relationship exists:** *"... that the patient is under the physician's care for the debilitating medical condition." Section 10(y)*.

Certifications for legitimate patients only

A physician may certify the use of medical cannabis only for individuals with whom he has a legitimate physician-patient relationship concerning the treatment of a debilitating medical condition. A physician may be sanctioned under the *Medical Practice Act* for certifying a person who is not under his care or does not have a debilitating medical condition." *Section 35(d)*.

Veterans and VA hospitals

With regard to forming the required patient-physician relationship to certify medical cannabis use, the law explicitly envisions the special cases of military veterans who receive health care services at VA hospitals.

Veterans receive written certifications from VA physicians in the same general manner as other patients:

> "A veteran who has received treatment at a VA hospital is deemed to have a bona fide physician-patient relationship with a VA physician if the patient has been seen for his or her debilitating medical condition at the VA Hospital in accordance with VA Hospital protocols. All reasonable i inferences regarding the existence of a bona fide physician-patient relationship shall be drawn in favor of an applicant who is a veteran and has undergone treatment at a VA hospital." Section 60(c).

In-person "physical examination" of patient is necessary

A physician must physically see a patient in person to certify that the patient has a debilitating medical condition. Under no circumstances may a physician conduct a certifying examination via remote technology. *Section 35(a)(3).*

Also, before issuing a certification, a physician must conduct a physical examination:

> "A written certification shall be made only in the course of a bona fide physician-patient relationship, after the physician has completed an assessment of the qualifying patient's medical history, reviewed relevant records related to the patient's debilitating medical condition, and conducted a physical examination." Section 10(y).

Recordkeeping

The law requires physicians to maintain records of all of the patients they certify for cannabis use. A physician must keep these records in a system that is accessible to and subject to review by the Department of Public Health and the Department of Financial and Professional Regulation. This information is otherwise confidential. *Section 35(a)(4).*

Physician's Standard of Conduct

The same standards and practices which generally determine the correctness of physicians' actions are applicable in the context of certifying patients with debilitating conditions. Physicians are expected to use their own sound professional judgment to diagnose debilitating medical conditions and recommend cannabis when appropriate. The explicit language of the law states:

> *"A physician making a medical cannabis recommendation shall comply with generally accepted standards of medical practice, the provisions of the Medical Practice Act of 1987 and all applicable rules."* Section 35(a)(2).

Naturally, if a physician were to err in his diagnosis, he could be disciplined and held legally liable to the same extent as a misdiagnosis or mistreatment in any other context. A physician's violation of the *Compassionate Use of Medical Cannabis Pilot Program Act* may be deemed a violation of the *Medical Practice Act* for purposes of disciplining a physician professionally. *Section 35(d)*.

Legal Immunities

Having been strictly prohibited for decades, cannabis is something generations of successful professionals have been conditioned to avoid. But if the medical profession and the medical cannabis industry are to function properly, then health care professionals must feel assured they can discuss cannabis without fearing legal or professional liability. One way the law accomplishes this is by explicitly promising that physicians are free from arrest, prosecution, professional reprimand, and other penalties when they recommend cannabis in the manner authorized by law.

Physicians are protected:

> *".. for providing written certifications or for otherwise*
> *stating that in the physician's professional opinion, a*
> *patient is likely to receive therapeutic or palliative benefit*
> *from the medical use of cannabis to treat or alleviate the*
> *patient's debilitating medical condition or symptoms*
> *associated with the debilitating medical condition."*
> Section 25(e).

In these circumstances, the physician shall not be subject to :

- arrest
- prosecution
- penalty in any manner
- denial of any right or privilege
- civil penalty
- disciplinary action by the Medical Disciplinary
  Board or any other professional licensing board.
  Section 25(e).

Immunities for bystanders

The law also gives explicit immunities to bystanders and individuals who assist a registered patient in administering medical cannabis, even if the individual is not a caregiver. *Section 25(f)(2-3).* This rule would apply in a health care facilities and elsewhere to protect doctors, nurses, and other health care providers who assist a patient in administering cannabis medicine.

PHYSICIANS' CONFLICTS OF INTEREST RULES

The law prohibits physicians from having incentive-based relationships with cultivation centers and dispensaries. When a physician recommends cannabis, it must be for reasons purely in the best interest of the patient.

No kickbacks: Other than the typical fee a physician collects from examining a patient, a physician may not accept money or anything else of value from a patient, caregiver, dispensary, or cultivation center. *Section 35(b)(1).*

No discount agreements: A physician may not offer discounts to a patient in exchange for the patient's agreement to use a particular caregiver or dispensary. *Section 35(b)(2).*

No seeing patients at dispensaries: A physician may not examine patients at a dispensary. A physician also may not examine patients at the home or office of a principal officer or employee of a cultivation center or dispensary. *Section 35(b)(3).*

No ownership in medical cannabis industry: A physician who certifies patients may not hold any ownership interest in a cultivation center or dispensary. The prohibition on ownership also applies to physicians who are engaged in partnerships or profit-sharing agreements with other physicians who certify patients. *Section 35(b)(4).* By implication, if a physician never intends to prescribe cannabis or partner with a physician who recommends cannabis, then the physician may be allowed to own an interest in a dispensary or cultivation center.

No working in medical cannabis industry: A physician may not volunteer or work as an employee of a cultivation center or dispensary. A physician may not serve on the board of directors of a cultivation center or dispensary. *Section 35(b)(5).*

No referrals to medical cannabis industry: A physician may not refer patients to a cultivation center, dispensary, or caregiver. *Section 35(b)(6).*

No advertising in dispensary or cultivation center: A physician may not advertise in a dispensary or cultivation center. *Section 35(b)(7).*

Cannabis Use at Health Care Facilities

The law generally tries to keep cannabis use out of view from the public, but health care facilities are a necessary exception because some medical cannabis patients will be hospitalized or otherwise checked into a health care facility from time to time. Although the law discourages the use of cannabis in public places, health care facilities are explicitly excluded from the law's special definition of "public places." *Section 30(a)(3)(F).*

"Health care facilities" includes but is not limited to:

- hospitals
- nursing homes
- hospice care centers
- long-term care facilities. *Section 30(a)(3)(F).*

Cannabis use permitted, but "smoking" prohibited

Registered patients may legally use medical cannabis products at health care facilities, but smoking cannabis is explicitly prohibited. *Section 30(a)(4).* The law does not specify whether "smoking" includes vaporizing. This question may be answered by the Department of Public Health's forthcoming regulations. *Section 165(b)(7).*

Further regulations forthcoming

The Department of Public Health is instructed to adopt regulations to determine the rules for cannabis use at health care facilities. Specifically:

> *"The Department of Public Health rules shall address... reasonable rules concerning the medical use of cannabis at a nursing care institution, hospice, assisted living center, assisted living facility, assisted living home, residential care institution, or adult day care facility." Section 165(b)(7).*

BECOMING A PATIENT
OR CAREGIVER

Subjects Covered:

- Debilitating medical conditions
- Obtaining a physician's written certification
- Caregivers
- Applying for a registry identification card
- Grounds for denial
- Using the registry identification card
- Protection of confidential information

The law tries as best it can to make sure only legitimately ill patients use cannabis. Patients must undergo a registration process to verify that they have a legitimate need for medical cannabis. The first part of the process entails forming a relationship with a licensed Illinois physician who diagnoses the patient as suffering from a "debilitating medical condition," as defined by the law. The physician must formally "certify" that the patient may be able to benefit from using cannabis. The second part of the process entails applying to become a cardholder in the Department of Public Health's registry identification system.

The law allows patients who are too disabled to visit a dispensary themselves to designate a caregiver to do so on their behalf. Caregivers are registered into the same registry identification database as patients and possess the same immunities related to possession of medical cannabis, but caregivers may not use medical cannabis.

Debilitating Medical Conditions

Before a patient may legally use or obtain medical cannabis, the patient must receive a diagnosis from a licensed physician indicating that the patient suffers from a specific illness appearing on the law's list of "debilitating medical conditions." *Section 10(t)*.

The full list of debilitating medical conditions appears on page 1 of this book.

Citizens may petition for expansion of list

The law gives the Department of Public Health power to expand the list of debilitating medical conditions so that more patients can qualify to obtain medical cannabis. As a matter of formality, the process must be initiated by an Illinois citizen rather than from within the agency itself. Any Illinois citizen may initiate the process by filing a petition requesting that the agency consider expanding the list. The petition must identify the particular condition that the patient would like to see added. The agency must acknowledge and consider the petition through a formal procedure requiring public notice and hearing, and it must approve or deny a petition within 180 days. *Section 45*.

Obtaining a Physician's Written Certification

Any "doctor of medicine or doctor of osteopathy" with licenses in good standing under the Illinois *Medical Practice Act*[28] and *Illinois Controlled Substances Act*[29] may issue an official certification for a patient. *Section 35(a)(1)*. The law explicitly does not authorize licensed practitioners under any other law, including *Illinois' Dental Practice Act*[30]. *Sections 10(s)*.

28. 225 ILCS 60/.
29. 720 ILCS 570/.
30. 225 ILCS 25.

Form of physician's written certification

The law instructs physicians to use an official form prepared by the Department of Public Health when recommending cannabis for patients with debilitating conditions. Patients must attach submit the physician's written certification form when they apply for a patient identification card. The written certification must not be dated more than 90 days priors to the application date. *Section 55(a)(1).*

Veterans and VA hospitals

With regard to forming the required patient-physician relationship to certify medical cannabis use, the law explicitly envisions the special cases of military veterans who receive health care services at a VA hospital. Veterans receive written certifications from VA physicians in the same general manner as other patients.

> *"A veteran who has received treatment at a VA hospital is deemed to have a bona fide physician-patient relationship with a VA physician if the patient has been seen for his or her debilitating medical condition at the VA Hospital in accordance with VA Hospital protocols. All reasonable inferences regarding the existence of a bona fide physician-patient relationship shall be drawn in favor of an applicant who is a veteran and has undergone treatment at a VA hospital." Section 60(c).*

CAREGIVERS

A patient with a debilitating medical condition may be so disabled that he cannot travel to a dispensary to purchase medical cannabis, even though he is validly registered to do so. The law accommodates a patient in a situation like this by allowing the patient to appoint a "designated caregiver" who may purchase cannabis from the patient's appointed dispensary on the patient's behalf. *Section 10(i).* A caregiver must apply for a registry identification card in the same manner that a patient does. A patient can have only one designated caregiver, and a caregiver can be designated for only one patient. *Sections 10(i), 55.*

A caregiver must meet these criteria:

1. Is at least 21 years of age.

2. Agrees to assist a patient's medical use of cannabis.

3. Has not been convicted of a violent crime or controlled substance felony.

4. Does not assist any other patient with medical use of cannabis. *Section 10(i).*

Caregiver's immunities

The law gives caregivers explicit assurances that they need not fear prosecution, arrest or other penalties for possessing cannabis after purchasing it on behalf of a registered patient. Caregivers also have express permission to assist patients if necessary.

Specifically:

> *"A registered designated caregiver is not subject to arrest, prosecution, or denial of any right or privilege, including but not limited to civil penalty or disciplinary action by an occupational or professional licensing board, for acting in accordance with this Act to assist a registered qualifying patient to whom he or she is connected through the Department [of Public Health]'s registration process with the medical use of cannabis."* Section 25(b).

The amount possessed by the caregiver plus the amount possessed by the patient may not exceed the patient's "adequate supply" limit of 2.5 ounces per 14-day period. *Section 25(b).*

APPLYING FOR A REGISTRY IDENTIFICATION CARD

After a patient's debilitating medical condition has been certified by a physician, the patient may apply for a registry identification card through the Department of Public Health. The agency oversees the application process and maintains a confidential list of patients and caregivers who have been issued registry identification cards. Patients and caregivers are entered into the same system and are governed by similar procedures. *Section 55(a)(1).* The agency may make the application process available via electronic submission. *Section 60(a)(4).*

State Police background investigation

Anyone applying to become registered as a patient or caregiver must undergo a background investigation performed by the Illinois State Police. Background investigations entail a state and federal criminal records check, and require the submission of fingerprint samples. *Section 65(d).*

No drug-related felony convictions

The Department of Public Health may deny a patient's application for a registry identification card if the patient has ever been convicted of a drug related felony. *Section 65(b).*

A patient or caregiver can be denied for felony convictions of:

- Illinois' *Controlled Substances Act*[31].
- Illinois' *Cannabis Control Act*[32].
- Illinois' *Methamphetamine Control and Community Protection Act*[33].
- A similar provision of a local ordinance or other jurisdiction. *Section 65(b).*

---

31. 720 ILCS 570/.
32. 720 ILCS 550/.
33. 720 ILCS 646/.

Medical care disclosures

When submitting an application, a patient must sign privacy waivers authorizing the Department of Public Health to obtain any information that is necessary to confirm the patient's medical background.

The Department of Public Health may seek and obtain information required to verify:

1. That the patient and physician have a bona-fide relationship.

2. That the patient is under the physician's care for the patient's debilitating medical condition.

3. To substantiate the patient's diagnosis. *Section 55(a)(2).*

Application fees may be needs-based

The law does not establish the amount of the application fees for patients and caregivers. Instead, the Department of Public Health is given authority to establish the amount of the fee through its forthcoming regulations. *Section 165(b)(1).*

The law instructs the agency that it may adopt a sliding scale of fees, whereby the amount varies depending on the patient's household income. The law also suggests that "The Department of Public Health may accept donations from private sources to reduce application and renewal fees. *Section 165(e).* Patients and caregivers are required to resubmit applications annually, and the agency must establish the amount of renewal fees as well. *Sections 70(c), 165(d)(1).*

Reimbursement for costs of cannabis use not required

The law explicitly does not require any government medical assistance program or private health insurer to reimburse a patient for costs of medical cannabis use:

> *"Nothing in this Act may be construed to require a government medical assistance program or private health insurer to reimburse a person for costs associated with the medical use of cannabis." Section 40(d).*

Additional fee for Health Dept's education function

In addition to registration and renewal fees, patients and caregivers must pay a completely separate fee, the proceeds of which shall be used to provide information about medical cannabis to the general public.

> "...[the fee] shall be used to develop and disseminate
> educational information about the health risks associated with
> the abuse of cannabis and prescription medicines."
> Section 165 (e).

The amount of the fee will be established by the Department of Public Health's forthcoming regulations. *Section 165(e).*

Patient's choice of designated dispensary

A registered patient may obtain permission to purchase cannabis products at only one dispensary. The patient is allowed to choose his designated dispensary and is requested to do so at the time he submits an application to the Department of Public Health. *Section 55(a)(7).*

A patient may later change to a different designated dispensary through a separate application process overseen by the Department of Public Health. *Section 75(e).* Or alternatively, a dispensary has the ability to help a patient process a change in his designated dispensary by contacting the agency to notify it that the patient wishes to change his designation. The agency may then adjust its verification database accordingly. *Section 135.*

Sworn promise not to resell medical cannabis

Along with an application to become a patient or caregiver, applicants must submit a signed statement "asserting that they will not divert medical cannabis." *Section 55(a)(8).*

Health Dept. Procedure for Approving or Denying

The law instructs the Department of Public Health to verify the information in a patient's application and make a decision approving or denying the application within 30 days of receiving it. *Section 60(a)(1).* Upon approving an application, the agency must issue a registry identification card to the patient within 15 business days. *Section 60(a)(2).*

Grounds for Denial

The Department of Public Health may (but need not necessarily) deny a qualified patient's application only if the application fails for any of the following specific reasons:

> • Patient did not provide all required information and materials.
> • Patient has already had a registry identification card previously revoked.
> • Patient does not meet the law's requirements.
> • Patient provided false information. *Section 65(a)(1-4).*
> • Patient has been convicted of a drug related felony. *Section 65(b).*

The Department of Public Health may (but need not necessarily) deny the application of a patient's chosen caregiver for any of the following specific reasons:

> • Caregiver did not provide all required information.
> • Caregiver has been convicted of a violent crime or controlled substance felony.
> • Prospective patient's application was denied.
> • Caregiver already had a registry identification card previously revoked.
> • Caregiver provided false information. *Section 65(a)(1-4).*
> • Caregiver has been convicted of a drug related felony. *Section 65(b).*

Denial is final agency action

When the Department of Public Health denies a prospective patient or caregiver's application or renewal, it is considered a "final Department action," which means there is no further means to raise objections with the agency, such as by appeal. At this point the appropriate venue for raising objections is the local Circuit Court. *Section 65(f).*

THE REGISTRY IDENTIFICATION CARD

The Department of Public Health issues registry identification cards to patients and caregivers whose applications it approves. *Section 60.* The following information shall appear on registry identification cards:

- Name of cardholder.
- Whether cardholder is a patient or caregiver.
- Date of issue.
- Date of expiration (one-year after date of issue).
- A random, unique alphanumeric identification number.
- If the card is for a caregiver, it will contain the random unique alphanumeric identification number of the patient.
- A photograph of the cardholder (if required by the Department of Public Health's regulations). *Section 70(b)(1-6).*

The law instructs the Department of Public Health that this information may be stored electronically on the card so that it can be read by law enforcement agents. *Section 70(e).* Storing data electronically would also enable dispensaries to read the data, which would make it very difficult to slip forged information past a dispensary.

Card must be on person while using cannabis

The law requires a patient or caregiver to have his registry identification card with him at all times when engaging in the use of medical cannabis. *Section 70(a).*

Duty to notify Health Dept of basic changes

Registered cardholders must notify the Department of Public Health within ten days of a change in any of the following:

- Name of the patient or caregiver.
- Address of the patient or caregiver.
- Medical condition of the patient.

Duty to report lost cards

A patient or caregiver must notify the Department of Public Health within 10 days of a registry identification card becoming lost or missing. The agency shall then issue a new card with a new random alphanumeric identification number within 15 days. *Sections 75(a)(4), 75(b).*

Changing caregivers

A patient who wishes to change his caregiver must notify the Department of Public Health beforehand. The new chosen caregiver must submit an application and undergo a criminal background investigation performed by the Illinois State Police, same as with the original caregiver. *Sections 55, 75(a)(3).*

Protection of Confidential Information

The law assures patients that private information about their health and medical decisions shall remain confidential. The law protects information that a patient or caregiver shares with physicians, the Department of Public Health, and dispensaries:

> **Application information:** The Department of Public Health must keep confidential: "applications and renewals, their contents, and supporting information submitted by qualifying patients and designated caregivers, including information regarding their designated caregivers and physicians." *Section 145(a)(1).*

> **Purchases:** Any information related to a patient or caregiver's purchases and other information obtained through a patient's interactions with a dispensary must be kept in confidence. *Section 145(a)(4).*

Medical records: "All medical records provided to the Department of Public Health in connection with an application for a registry card" must be kept in confidence. *Section 145(a)(5).*

These records are confidential, but the Department of Public Health, Department of Financial and Professional Regulation, Department of Agriculture, and the Illinois State Police "may disclose this information and records to each other upon request." *Section145(a).*

Breach of a patient or caregiver's confidential information is a Class B misdemeanor punishable by a fine of $1,000, regardless if the breacher is an employee of a dispensary or one of Illinois' administrative agencies. *Section 145(c).*

Using Medical Cannabis Legally

Subject Covered:

- Terms related to cannabis use

- Rules of possessing medical cannabis

- Rules of using medical cannabis

- Traffic safety

- Cannabis in the workplace

- Active duty officers and transportation workers

- Freedom from discrimination

- Immunities and presumptions

The *Compassionate Use of Medical Cannabis Pilot Program Act* helps patients finally obtain cheap, effective treatment for certain medical conditions, but it also recognizes that cannabis has psychoactive properties that can impair patients' behavior, concentration, and ability to perform every day tasks. And generally, more patients being affected by cannabis means more patients causing accidents that affect other people. The law therefore seeks to strike a balance between allowing patients access to good medicine and protecting society at large from mistakes patients could make after taking their medicine.

The law's solution is to impose restrictions on the ways and places patients may consume cannabis. Generally, the law tries to push cannabis use away from areas where accidents may be common or costly, such as traffic and the workplace. The law also wants to keep cannabis out of public sight, and especially away from children. Meanwhile employers, colleges, and landlords are given protections for their businesses and property, but no one may discriminate against another person for being registered as a patient or caregiver.

Terms Related to Cannabis Use

It is important to distinguish between different types of conduct related to cannabis because one type of conduct may be OK in a particular setting while another is not.

Smoking

Smoking generally entails rolling cannabis buds into cigarette paper or putting them into a pipe in order to burn the plant material and inhale the smoke. Smoking is the least preferred method of cannabis use under the law. In addition to laboring the lungs, smoking creates secondhand smoke and produces an odor.

In some situations the law prohibits smoking but would otherwise allow a patient to use cannabis some other way. Smoking is explicitly banned at health care facilities, for example, but ingesting a cannabis-infused product or edible is not. *Section 30(a)(4)*.

Vaporizing

Vaporizing is somewhat like smoking but there are important differences. Vaporizing entails putting cannabis buds into an apparatus which heats the plant material but does not apply a burning flame. It is enough heat to break down the plant material so that cannabinoids are released, but not so much heat that the plant material combusts and burns. Cannabinoids are thereby inhaled as vapor rather than smoke. Vaporizing is healthier than smoking because it labors the lungs less. Vaporizing also does not produce a strong odor or expose bystanders to secondhand smoke.

The law does not address vaporizing, which means there is no clear guidance yet whether vaporizing will be prohibited to the same extent as smoking. For example, it is not clear whether the prohibition on smoking cannabis in health care facilities means a person also may not vaporize cannabis in a health care facility. The Department of Public Health may adopt regulations addressing the question or otherwise provide guidance. *Section 165(b)(7)*.

Impaired

Whether a patient is impaired is a conclusion based on evidence of surrounding circumstances. It is a conclusion typically made by law enforcement officers, employers, regulatory agencies, and the courts after an accident or dispute has already happened. Evidence of impairment usually relates to changes in appearance and behavior. A patient is not necessarily impaired every time he uses cannabis, just like a person is not necessarily impaired every time he uses alcohol. The law prohibits a patient from operating a motor vehicle or engaging in other potentially dangerous activity if he is impaired by medical cannabis. The rules are similar to the rules for safe alcohol use.

To possess

To possess cannabis means to carry it on one's self or in a pocket, bag, purse, container, vehicle, etc. which the patient has control over. Possessing cannabis is not the same as using it. A patient can legally possess medical cannabis in places where he may not legally use it.

To use

Using cannabis entails the physical act of consuming cannabis by smoking or ingesting it. The use of cannabis endures for as long as the patient may be psychoactively impaired. For example, if a patient were to smoke cannabis at home and then get into a vehicle and drive, he may be using cannabis illegally in traffic, even if he has not taken any cannabis with him.

Adequate supply

"Adequate supply" refers to the maximum legal amount of cannabis a registered patient or his designated caregiver may purchase. The adequate supply limit is 2.5 ounces of cannabis during a 14-day period. *Section 10(a)(1).*

Pre-mixed weight

"Pre-mixed weight" refers to the weight of cannabis used to make a cannabis infused product or edible. Compared to the amount of cannabis that must be smoked to get the intended effect, a substantially larger amount of cannabis is needed to produce infused products and edibles. The law's adequate supply of 2.5 ounces is much more than any one patient could smoke by himself in a 14-day period. But with regard to the pre-mixed weight of infused products, 2.5 ounces is a much more appropriate limit.

Rules of
Possessing Medical Cannabis

In an effort to reduce accidents and other social costs, the law imposes restrictions on the places patients and caregivers are authorized to possess cannabis.

Places where cannabis possession not permitted

The law explicitly lists several places where a patient or caregiver is not authorized to possess cannabis:

- On a school bus
- On the grounds of a preschool
- On the grounds of a primary school
- On the grounds of a secondary school
- In a residence where child care or similar services are performed.
- In a correctional facility
- In a motor vehicle upon a highway in Illinois unless the cannabis is still in its original unopened package.
- In a vehicle not open to the public unless the cannabis is in a reasonably secured, sealed, tamper-evident container and reasonably inaccessible while the vehicle is moving. *Section 30(a)(2)(A-F).*

Card must be on person while using cannabis

The law requires patients and caregivers to have their registry identification cards with them at all times when using or possessing medical cannabis. *Section 70(a).*

Cardholder may not possess more than adequate supply

A cardholder may not intentionally obtain or by other means possess an amount of cannabis that would exceed the adequate supply of 2.5 ounces per 14-day period. The penalty is revocation of the patient or caregiver's registry identification card, in addition to other possible charges. *Section 30(g)*.

RULES OF USING MEDICAL CANNABIS

Another part of reducing accidents and social costs entails restricting the ways and places a patient may consume cannabis. Naturally, the law is more restrictive about where a patient may use cannabis compared to where he may possess it. Additionally, other parties with rights or interests in maintaining property are given protections against patients' misuse of cannabis. For example, private business owners can restrict or prohibit altogether the use of cannabis, and landlords can prevent the use of smoking in their property.

Cannabis use not permitted in a "public place"

The law wants patients to use cannabis in private settings, not out in open public. The law uses a special definition of "public place" to explain the settings where patients are not authorized to use cannabis. The special definition defines a public place as:

> *"...any place where an individual could reasonably be expected to be observed by others." Section 30(a)(3)(F).*

The definition of "public place" is modified to address the following types of places:

> **Government buildings (included):** A public place "includes all parts of buildings owned in whole or in part, or leased, by the State or a local unit of government."

Private residences (not included): A public place does not include a private residence unless the private residence is used to provide "licensed child care, foster care, or other similar social service care on the premises."

Health care facilities (not included): A public place does not include a "health care facility," which includes but is not limited to:

- hospitals
- nursing homes
- hospice care centers
- long-term care facilities

Section 30(a)(3)(F) for all.

Other places where cannabis use is prohibited

In addition to discouraging cannabis use in "public places," the law lists several other specific places where patients are not authorized to use cannabis.

Using cannabis is prohibited:

- Knowingly in close proximity to anyone under the age of 18.
- In a school bus.
- On the grounds of a preschool.
- On the grounds of a primary school.
- On the grounds of a secondary school.
- In any correctional facility.
- In any motor vehicle.
- In any private residence that is used at any time to provide licensed child care or other similar social service care on the premises. *Section 30(a)(3)(A-E, G)*

Private business may restrict or prohibit cannabis use

Some parties have the right to make rules restricting or altogether prohibiting the use of medical cannabis on their property. This explicitly includes "private businesses."

> *"Nothing is this Act shall prevent a private business from restricting or prohibiting the medical use of cannabis on its property." Section 30(h).*

"Private businesses" is a broad class. It includes bars, restaurants, entertainment venues, retail and grocery stores, and generally most places that are open to the public. The law does not provide private businesses with guidance as to how they may enforce their workplace policies regarding medical cannabis use, but rules could be forthcoming from the Department of Public Health's pending regulations. *Section 165(b)(6).*

Some specific parties are given explicit rights to control patients' use of medical cannabis:

> **Universities:** "Universities, colleges, and other institutions of post-secondary education" may restrict or prohibit a patient's use of medical cannabis on their property. *Section 30(i).* But no school may discriminate by penalizing a student or refusing to enroll a prospective student based solely on the person's status as a registered patient or caregiver. *Section 40(a)(1).* No school may be penalized or denied any right under state law for enrolling, leasing to, or employing a cardholder. *Section 40(c).*

> **Landlords:** Landlords do not have the right to prohibit a patient's cannabis use altogether, but they do have the right to prohibit the smoking of cannabis in their properties. *Section 40(a)(1).* A landlord may not discriminate by penalizing a tenant or by refusing to lease to a prospective tenant based solely on the tenant's status as a registered patient or caregiver. *Section 40(a)(1).* No landlord may be penalized or denied any benefit under State law for leasing to a registered patient or caregiver. *Section 40(c).*

Employers: Employers may make reasonable workplace policies restricting or prohibiting a patient's use of cannabis. *Section 50*. An employer may not discriminate by penalizing an employee or refusing to hire a prospective employee based solely on the employee's status as a registered patient or caregiver. *Section 40(a)(1)*. No employer may be penalized or denied any benefit under state law for employing a patient or caregiver. *Section 40(c)*.

Prohibited activities while under the influence

The law tries to deter patients from undertaking certain activities while impaired. Specifically:

> *"This law does not permit any person to engage in, and does not prevent the imposition of any civil, criminal, or penalties for... undertaking any task under the influence of cannabis, when doing so would constitute negligence, professional malpractice, or professional misconduct." Section 30(a)(1).*

Additionally, the law amends the *Illinois Vehicle Code*[34] in various places to prohibit the operation of a motor vehicle while under the influence of cannabis. For practical purposes, the rules are very similar to the rules for alcohol use and motor vehicles. *Section 935*.

Cardholder cannot allow anyone else to use cannabis

A patient or caregiver may not allow any other person to use medical cannabis. *Section 30(a)(7)*. A cardholder may not sell or transfer cannabis to another person. *Section 30(a)(8)*.

Petty fines for lying to a physician or enforcement officer

It is a petty offense punishable by a fine of up to $1,000 to knowingly make a misrepresentation to a law enforcement official about medical marijuana use in an attempt to avoid arrest or prosecution. *Section 30(c)*. It is also a petty offense punishable by a fine of up to $1,000 to make a misrepresentation to a physician for the purpose of obtaining a written certification from the physician. *Section 30(d)*.

34. 625 ILCS 5/.

Active Duty Officers And Transportation Workers

The law does not permit the use of medical cannabis by any:

- Active duty law enforcement officer.
- Active duty correctional officer.
- Active duty correctional probation officer.
- Active duty firefighter. *Section 30(a)(9).*
- Person with a school bus permit.
- Person with a Commercial Driver's License. *Section 30(a)(10).*

TRAFFIC
SAFETY

Recognizing that cannabis can have impairing effects on patients, the law imposes rules forbidding the use of cannabis in motorized vehicles. The law makes several amendments to the *Illinois Vehicle Code*[35] to create rules that prohibit patients from operating vehicles while under the influence of medical cannabis. Generally, a patient may not commit the act of smoking or ingesting cannabis prior to or while operating a motorized vehicle, boat, or plane. Nor may the patient operate a vehicle while impaired.

Secretary of State's notation on driving record

Whenever the Department of Public Health approves a patient or caregiver's application for a registry identification card, the agency must forward the person's driver registration number to the Secretary of State, which shall then make a notation on the person's driving record. *Section 60(d).*

Negligence rules

One of the rules that operates to deter the use of cannabis in traffic is the rule that holds patients liable for negligence when they

35. 625 ILCS 5/.

undertake activities while under the influence:

> "This Act does not permit any person to engage in...
> Undertaking any task under the influence of cannabis, when
> doing so would constitute negligence, professional malpractice,
> or professional misconduct. Section 30(a)(1).

This rule provides a means to hold the patient accountable for the costs of accidents and other losses he may cause as a result of undertaking activities while under the influence. In some cases criminal charges may also apply under other provisions of the law, such as the *Vehicle Code* amendments.

No operating vehicles, aircraft, or motorboats

In addition to making several amendments to Illinois' *Vehicle Code*, the law includes an explicit provision prohibiting patients from operating vehicles while under the influence:

> "This Act does not permit any person to engage in...
> Operating, navigating, or being in actual physical control of
> any motor vehicle, aircraft, or motorboat while using or under
> the influence of cannabis in violation of Sections 11-501 and
> 11-502.1 of the Illinois Vehicle Code. Section 30(a)(5).

No use by persons with certain transportation jobs

The law prohibits the use of any medical cannabis whatsoever by any person with a school bus permit or Commercial Driver's License. This rule does not simply apply only when the person is working; a person with a school bus permit or Commercial Driver's License may never use medical cannabis *Section 30(a)(10)*.

Penalty for cannabis DUI is revocation of card

One of the law's amendments to the *Vehicle Code* is a new section (*625 ILCS 5/11-502.1*: "Possession of medical cannabis in a motor vehicle.") which prohibits the use and possession of cannabis by anyone, driver or passenger, in a motor vehicle. The penalty for such a violation is revocation of the patient's registry identification card.

"Any registered qualifying patient who commits a violation of Section 11-502.1 of the Illinois Vehicle Code or refuses a properly requested test related to operating a motor vehicle while under the influence of cannabis shall have his or her registry identification card revoked. Section 30(f).

Vehicle Code Amendments

The *Compassionate Use of Medical Cannabis Pilot Program Act* makes substantial amendments to the *Illinois Vehicle Code*. Generally the rules for medical cannabis are analogous to those for alcohol.

The *Vehicle Code (625 ILCS 5/)* is amended in the following places:

> • Section 2-118.1: "Opportunity for hearing; statutory summary alcohol or other drug related suspension or revocation pursuant to Section 11-501.1."
> • Section 6-206: "Discretionary authority to suspend or revoke license or permit; Right to hearing."
> • Section 6-206.1: "Monitoring Device Driving Permit; Declaration of Policy."
> • Section 6-208.1: "Period of statutory summary alcohol, other drug, or intoxicating compound related suspension or revocation."
> • Section 6-514: "Commercial Driver's License (CDL) Disqualifications."
> • Section 11-501: "Driving while under the influence of alcohol, other drug or drugs, intoxicating compound or compounds or any combination thereof."
> • Section 11-501.1: "Suspension of driver's license; statutory summary alcohol, other drug or drugs, or intoxicating compound or compounds related suspension or revocation; implied consent."
> • Section 11-501.2: "Chemical and other tests."
> *Section 935 for all.*

The law also adds to the *Vehicle Code* a new Section 11-502.1: "Possession of medical cannabis in a motor vehicle." *Section 935.*

CANNABIS
IN THE WORKPLACE

The law appreciates employers' concerns that increased cannabis use could have a negative effect on workers' productivity levels and frequency of accidents.

Employer's reasonable workplace rules

The law gives employers the right to make "reasonable" rules concerning the use of medical cannabis at work. Specifically, the law states that:

> *"Nothing is this Act shall prohibit an employer from adopting reasonable regulations concerning the consumption, storage, or timekeeping requirements for qualifying patients related to the use of medical cannabis." Section 50(a).*

The law does not define what is "reasonable" in this context. Generally questions about what is "reasonable" are settled by administrative agencies and courts. The law does explicitly indicate that an employer can enforce "a policy concerning drug testing, zero-tolerance, or a drug free workplace provided the policy is applied in a nondiscriminatory manner." *Section 50(b).*

When is an employee impaired?

Determining if an employee is impaired is important because an employer's workplace policies would be wise to state that performing work activities while impaired is a punishable violation. The law provides some guidance in this area by stating that an employer may consider an employee to be impaired whenever a range of symptoms are manifested in the employee.

An employer may deem an employee impaired if the employee:

*"manifests specific, articulable symptoms while working
that decrease or lessen his or her performance of the duties
or tasks of the employee's job position." Section 50(f).*

The law then lists the following as items in which changes can be
evidence of an impaired employee:

- speech
- physical dexterity
- agility
- coordination
- demeanor
- irrational or unusual behavior
- negligence
- carelessness in operating equipment or machinery
- disregard for the safety of the employee or others
- involvement in an accident that results in serious damage
  to equipment or property
- disruption of a production or manufacturing process
- carelessness that results in any injury to the employee or
  others. *Section 50(f).*

If an employer intends to discipline an employee after deciding
that the employee was impaired at work in violation of its workplace
policies, then the employer must allow the employee a reasonable
opportunity to contest the basis of the finding. *Section 50(f).*

Licensed professional's use of medical cannabis

In the case of licensed professionals who may not answer to a
supervisor or employer, medical cannabis use is not necessarily
prohibited while working. Licensed professionals enjoy discretion to
manage their own cannabis use in a way that does not affect their work.
But of course if a licensed professional were to use medical cannabis
and then cause a mistake or accident as a result of impairment, then
he may be held liable for negligence and professional misconduct.
Section 25(a).

"Licensed professionals" are explicitly given immunity from arrest, prosecution, and other civil and professional penalties to the same extent as all other patients-- even when using cannabis while practicing their profession-- but not if impaired:

> *"A registered qualifying patient is not subject to arrest, prosecution, or denial of any right or privilege... where the registered qualifying patient is a licensed professional, the use of cannabis does not impair that licensed professional when he or she is engaged in the practice of the profession for which he or she is licensed. Section 25(a).*

Freedom
from Discrimination

The law takes care to assure patients and caregivers who comply with the law that they should not fear social or economic disincentives. One way the law protects them is by prohibiting discrimination. No party may treat a patient or caregiver differently because they are registered as a cardholder. Specifically:

> *"No school, employer, or landlord may refuse to enroll or lease to, or otherwise penalize, a person solely for his or her status as a registered qualifying patient or a registered designated caregiver, unless failing to do so would put the school, employer, or landlord in violation of federal law or unless failing to do so would cause it to lose a monetary or licensing-related benefit under federal law or rules..."*
> *Section 40(a)(1).*

No negative consequences for organ transplant recipients

A registered patient's legal use of medical cannabis is considered no different that the legal use of any other pharmaceutical or prescription drug. A patient shall not be denied medical treatment on the basis of being a user of medical cannabis:

"For the purposes of medical care, including organ transplants, a registered qualifying patient's authorized use of cannabis in accordance with this Act is considered the equivalent of the authorized use of any other medication used at the direction of a physician, and may not constitute the use of an illicit substance or otherwise disqualify a patient from needed medical care. "Section 40(a)(2).

No negative consequences for child custody

A registered patient may not be denied custody or visitation rights with a minor simply because the patient uses legal medical cannabis:

"A person otherwise entitled to custody of or visitation or parenting time with a minor may not be denied that right, and there is no presumption of neglect or child endangerment, for conduct allowed under this Act, unless the person's actions in relation to cannabis were such that they created an unreasonable danger to the safety of the minor as established by clear and convincing evidence." Section 40(b).

Colleges and universities

A school may not penalize or refuse to enroll a student solely because of the student's status as a registered patient or caregiver. *Section 40(a)(1).* No school may be penalized or denied any benefit under State law for enrolling a student who is cardholder. *Section 40(c).*

Employers

An employer may not penalize an employee or prospective employee solely because of the person's status as a registered patient or caregiver. *Section 40(a)(1).* No employer may be penalized or denied any benefit under State law for employing an employee who is a registered cardholder. *Section 40(c).*

Landlords

A landlord may not refuse to lease to a prospective tenant or otherwise penalize a tenant solely because of the tenant's status as a registered patient or caregiver. *Section 40(a)*. A landlord may, however, prohibit the smoking of cannabis on the property. *Section 40(a)(1)*. No landlord may be penalized or denied any benefit under State law for leasing to a tenant who is a registered cardholder. *Section 40(c)*.

IMMUNITIES AND PRESUMPTIONS

The law makes explicit promises to patients and caregivers that they shall be free from prosecution, arrest, and other penalties when they use medical cannabis in authorized ways.

Patient immunities

As long as a patient conforms to the law's rules related to use and possession of medical cannabis, the patient shall not be subject to:

- arrest
- prosecution
- denial of a right or privilege
- civil penalty
- disciplinary action by an occupational or professional licensing board. *Section 25(a)*.

Caregiver and bystander immunities

Caregivers and other bystanders are explicitly immune from sanction for being in the presence or vicinity of legitimate medical cannabis use and for assisting a patient in taking medical cannabis. *Section 25(b),(f)(2-3)*.

Presumption of compliance

The law creates a legal presumption that patients and caregivers are in compliance with the law if they possesses a valid patient identification card and not more than an "adequate supply" of cannabis. A legal presumption operates in court by imposing a burden on the prosecutor to produce evidence that the patient or caregiver was not in compliance with the law. If the prosecutor cannot meet this burden, the case fails.

In order to rebut the presumption and present a case, a prosecutor would have to show:

> *"...evidence that conduct related to cannabis was not for the purpose of treating or alleviating the qualifying patient's debilitating medical condition or symptoms associated with the debilitating medical condition in compliance with this Act." Section 25(d)*

PROTECTIONS FOR BUSINESSES, LANDLORDS & UNIVERSITIES

Subjects Covered:

- Employers

- Landlords

- Private Businesses and Places Open to the Public

- Universities

One problem with legalized medical cannabis use is that it potentially exposes society to more risks of accidents. More people using cannabis generally means more people becoming psychoactively affected by THC and sometimes going out into public and causing accidents.

In some circumstances the law protects certain parties from potential legal liability for accidents caused by patients impaired by cannabis. Employers, for example, can prohibit employees from using cannabis at work by adopting appropriate workplace policies. So then if an employee causes an accident after using cannabis in violation of the workplace policies, the employer may be protected from some of the legal costs of the accident. The law also gives residential landlords the right to prohibit tenants from smoking cannabis in their properties. Giving these protections is the law's way of balancing patients' need for good medicine against the rest of society's desire to avoid accidents and loss.

EMPLOYERS

Employers may be concerned about legalized medical cannabis use because they rely on the workers they hire to be productive and accident free. Impairment and psychoactive stimulation are generally not conducive to good work in most professions.

The law helps employers in a few ways. General prohibitions on using cannabis in public places and while performing particular activities (such as driving or operating heavy machinery) should serve some deterring effect. *Section 30(a)(3)*. The law also gives private businesses the right to restrict or prohibit the use of medical cannabis on their property. *Section 30(h)*.

But most importantly, the law allows employers to implement workplace policies which could protect the employer from legal liability in the event an employee commits an accident after becoming impaired by medical cannabis in violation of the workplace polices.

Reasonable workplace policies

The law allows employers to make and enforce workplaces policies related to the use of cannabis. The workplace policies may restrict and prohibit the use of cannabis at work, even for employees who are otherwise registered to legally use cannabis for medical purposes:

> *"Nothing in this Act shall prohibit an employer from adopting reasonable regulations concerning the consumption, storage, or timekeeping requirements for qualifying patients related to the use of medical cannabis." Section 50(a).*

Rules related to cannabis use can be part of an employer's overall zero tolerance drug and alcohol program, as long as they are applied in a consistent and nondiscriminatory manner. Testing for cannabis and other drugs can also be part of the workplace policies. *Section 50(b)*

Right to Discipline

An employer may discipline an employee for violating its workplace policies related to cannabis to the same extent it may discipline employees for other violations of its workplace policies. *Section 50(c)*. It is no defense for an employee that he obtained the medical cannabis legally. *Section 50(e)*.

When is a patient impaired at work?

Determining when an employee is impaired is a critical question because being impaired is conduct for which an employer may allege an employee has violated its workplace policies. If there is no physical evidence that the employee used cannabis immediately prior to an incident, then impairment may have to be inferred based upon the employee's behavior.

The law suggests an employer may generally consider an employee impaired if the employee:

> *"...manifests specific, articulable symptoms while working that decrease or lessen his or her performance of the duties or tasks of the employee's job position." Section 50(f).*

The law lists the following as items in which changes can be evidence of an impaired employee:

- speech
- physical dexterity
- agility
- coordination
- demeanor
- irrational or unusual behavior
- negligence
- carelessness in operating equipment or machinery
- disregard for the safety of the employee or others
- involvement in an accident that results in serious damage to equipment or property
- disruption of a production or manufacturing process
- carelessness that results in any injury to the employee or others. *Section 50(f).*

Disciplining employees for being impaired

The law allows an employer to discipline an employee after it makes a finding that the employee was impaired at work. However, the employer may not discipline an employee without first allowing the employee a reasonable opportunity to contest the basis of the finding. *Section 50(f).*

No new cause of action for disciplining employee

The law explicitly does not create a new cause of action resulting from the situation where a employer disciplines an employee after making a good faith finding that the employee used, possessed, or was impaired by medical cannabis at work. *Section 50(g)(1-2)*. Other causes of action in tort may still exist to remedy an employee or other party who suffers a loss through some fault of the employer.

Freedom from liability for employee accidents

The law explicitly states that it does not create a new cause of action resulting from the situation where an employee causes injury to a third party while impaired by cannabis, but the employer had no reason to know that its employee was impaired:

> *"Nothing in this Act shall be construed to create or imply a cause of action for any person against an employer for... injury or loss to a third party if the employer neither knew nor had reason to know that the employee was impaired."*
> *Section 50(g)(3).*

The implication of this provision may be that an employer may sometimes be able to avoid vicarious liability for accidents caused by employees impaired by cannabis.

No interference with transportation industry testing

The law specifies that transportation industry employers that are subject to the US Department of Transportation's regulation *49 CFR 40.151(e)*[36] shall not experience changes in the rules regarding workplace policies and drug testing *Section 50(h)*.

---

36. *49 CFR Section 40* deals with "Procedures for Transportation Workplace Drug and Alcohol Testing Programs"; *Subsection 151* is "What are MROs [Medical Review Officers] prohibited from doing as part of the review process?"

Active Duty Officers And Transportation Workers

The law does not permit the use of medical cannabis by any:

- Active duty law enforcement officer.
- Active duty correctional officer.
- Active duty correctional probation officer.
- Active duty firefighter. *Section 30(a)(9).*
- Person with a school bus permit.
- Person with a Commercial Driver's License. *Section 30(a)(10).*

No penalty for employing patients or caregivers

The law explicitly states that "No... employer may be penalized or denied any benefit under State law for... employing a cardholder." *Section 40(c).*

No discrimination against patients and caregivers

The law prohibits employers from penalizing an employee or refusing to hire a prospective employee "solely for his or her status as a registered qualifying patient or a registered designated caregiver." However, an employee may penalize an employee or refuse to hire a prospective employee if "failing to do so would cause [the employer] to lose a monetary or licensing-related benefit under federal law or rules." *Section 40(a)(1).*

LANDLORDS

The law recognizes that residential landlords may be exposed to increased risk because medical cannabis patients are encouraged to use cannabis primarily at home. However, the law is not particularly concerned about making new rules to cover property damage and other accidents caused by patients impaired by cannabis. Other bodies of law handle these scenarios well already. Lease agreements and the rules of landlord-tenant law, for example, generally hold the tenant liable for damage he causes to the property, regardless if he was impaired when he caused the damage.

Landlord may prohibit smoking cannabis but not using it

A landlord may not prohibit registered patients from using medical cannabis in his property, but he can prohibit patients from smoking cannabis in the property. *Section 40(a)(1).*

No discrimination against patients and caregivers

A landlord may not penalize a tenant or refuse to lease to a prospective tenant solely because the person is registered as a patient or caregiver, "unless failing to do so would put the... landlord in violation of federal law or unless failing to do so would cause it to lose a monetary or licensing-related benefit under federal law or rules." *Section 40(a)(1).*

PRIVATE BUSINESSES AND PLACES OPEN TO THE PUBLIC

For many types of businesses, employees are not the likeliest people to cause accidents. Business that are open to the general public, including bars, restaurants, churches, retail and grocery stores, entertainment venues, etc., are generally certain to experience more cannabis users coming onto their property. The law responds to the concerns of private businesses by giving them the right to restrict or prohibit altogether the use of medical cannabis on their property:

> *"Nothing in this Act shall prevent a private business from restricting or prohibiting the medical use of cannabis on its property." Section 30(h).*

The law does not provide private businesses with guidance as to how they may enforce their restrictions on cannabis use, but generally a private business would have the right to remove a person who does not comply with its rules. The Department of Public Health may provide further guidance in its forthcoming regulations. *Section 165(b)(6).*

Cannabis use discouraged in public places

Even if private businesses' were not granted the right to restrict and prohibit cannabis use on their property, cannabis use would still be unauthorized in most places of business. The law explicitly states that patients are not authorized to used cannabis in public places, defined partly as:

> *"...any place where an individual could reasonably be expected to be observed by others." Section 30(a)(3)(F).*

The law modifies its definition of "public places" to explicitly include government buildings and to explicitly exclude health care facilities and private residences (unless used for child care). Most private businesses also "public places," and hence a patient is not authorized to use cannabis on the property. A person who uses cannabis in a public place could face potential criminal charges based on using cannabis in a way that is not authorized by law.

COLLEGES AND UNIVERSITIES

The law gives colleges and universities the right to control medical cannabis use on their property to the same extent a private business may.

Right to restrict or prohibit cannabis use

Colleges and universities have the right to restrict or prohibit cannabis use on their property. The law does not provide guidance about how schools may go about enforcing their policies though:

"Nothing in this Act shall prevent a university, college, or other institution of post-secondary education from restricting or prohibiting the medical use of cannabis on its property." Section 30(i).

No discrimination against patients and caregivers

The law informs colleges and universities that they may not penalize a current student or refuse to enroll a prospective student solely because they are a patient or caregiver. *Section 40(a)(1)*. It also states that no college or university "may be penalized or denied any benefit under State law" for enrolling a patient or caregiver. Section 40(c). But beyond that the law does not provide guidance as to whether a school may or may not use an applicant's status as a patient or caregiver as part of a weight criteria formula for accepting new students.

About the author

Author Bradley Vallerius is an Illinois attorney and consultant focused on issues created by Illinois' *Compassionate Use of Medical Cannabis Pilot Program Act.* He helps businesses and individuals throughout Illinois understand how they can prepare for-- and in some cases take advantage of-- coming changes.

Bradley is a vastly experienced writer and communicator who is adept at monitoring legal issues in controversial new industries, having previously worked as a reporter and trade show producer in the global online gambling industry. Bradley is a graduate of Washington University in St. Louis (B.A., English, 2003) and Saint Louis University School of Law (J.D., 2011). Presently headquartered in Gillespie, Macoupin County, Illinois, Bradley travels to all parts of the state to help clients.

www.MedicalMarijuanaLawIllinois.com
information for cannabis industry professionals

31975664R00076

Made in the USA
Charleston, SC
03 August 2014